21 KEYS TO GETTING ANYTHING YOU WANT

BY

CHRISTIAN GEORG SCHWARZ

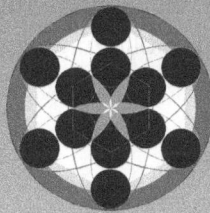

Bibliographic information from the Deutsche Nationalbibliothek:

The Deutsche Nationalbibliothek registers this publication in the German national bibliography, detailed bibliographical data is available online at http://dnb.dnb.de

Engineered Success – Turn your Vision into Profit

Kolpingweg 3, 85570 Markt Schwaben, Germany

info@christianschwarz.net

www.christianschwarz.net

www.facebook.com/engineeredsuccess

Photographs and diagrams without other names by Christian Georg Schwarz

ISBN 13 for printbook: 978-3-945912-02-7

Download here: www.christianschwarz.net/buecher

THE AUTHOR

Christian Georg Schwarz is entrepreneur, project developer, speaker, author and coach.

His motto "When they said sit down, I stood up" stands for going ones own individual path, finding solutions and realizing visions. Even on things where others claim that there is no possibility.

In the year 1998, as a freshly trained and graduated construction engineer – and despite all gloomy predicition – he founded a construction management company.

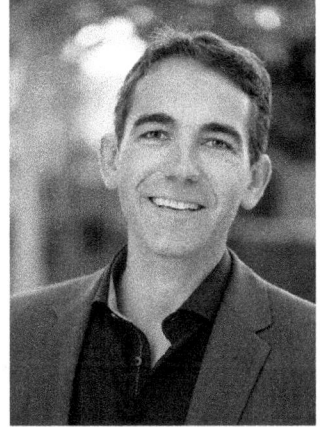

He sold it – once again, despite all well–meant advises – after 12 years of management, in order to focus even more on the sector consultation and lecture services.

His professional expertise is optimized by a considerable amount of national and international training, inter alia from Tony Robbins and JT Foxx so that he knows perfectly well how to bring a synergy into innovation, efficiency and leadership.

The impressions and lectures Christian Georg Schwarz could gather on ca. 30 individual tours, as well as the experiences as a father of three children serve next to his expertise, as an inspiring source for his work.

In this book, Christian Georg Schwarz presents a down–to–ground, but also a creative system that will help you, step by step, to turn your visions promptly into profit. Whether you define your "profit" as money, health, joy or the sum of it altogether and regardless of what challenges you meet in your professional or private life.

In this book, you receive 21 keys to getting anything you want.

TABLE OF CONTENTS

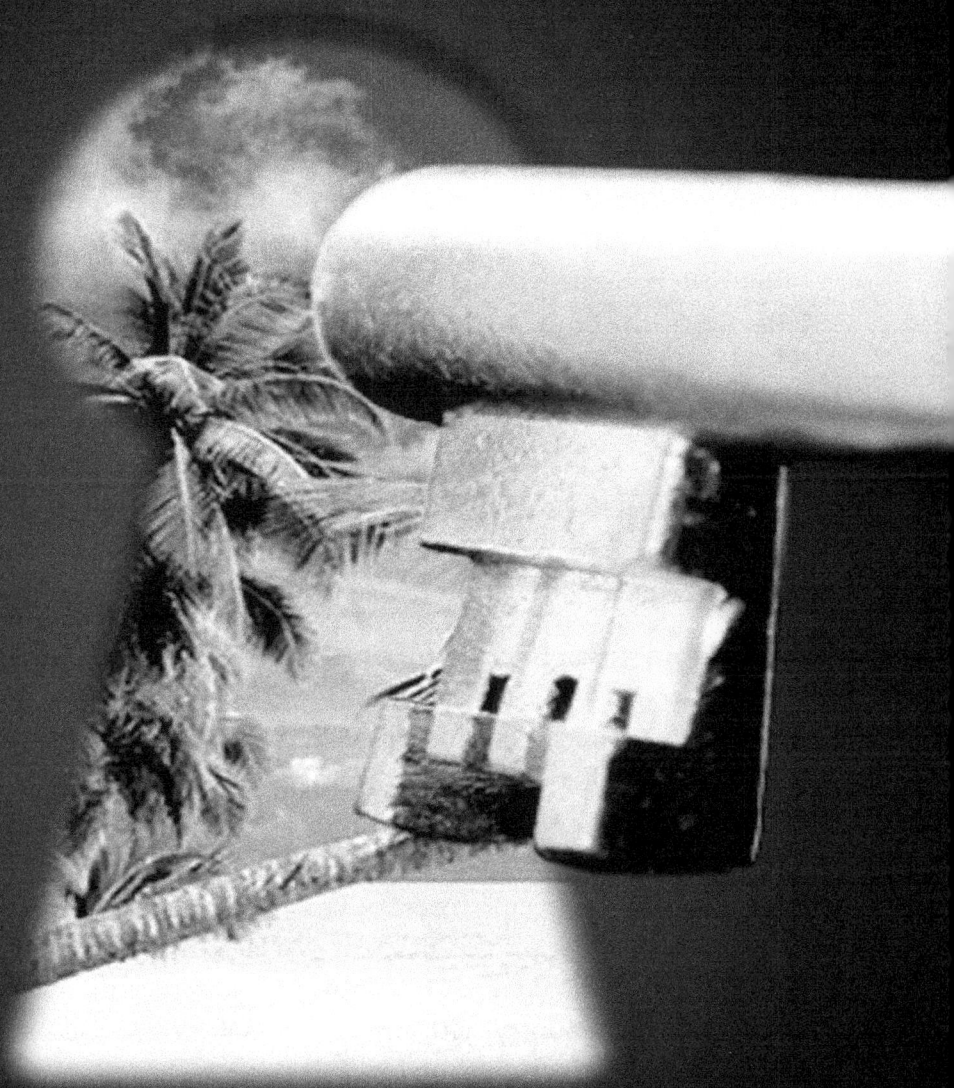

INTRODUCTION

"I will not work at Siemens from morning to evening until I am 60 years old, just to get hit by a car". That's what I told my father when I was 16 years old. Back then, I didn't know just how right I was: My father died ten years later in a car accident, aged 60. It happened two weeks after the start of his early retirement. The already booked trip to the mountains of the Karakorum, one of my father's life dreams remained a dream.

My father spent 30 years in an office. He was rarely home so that I can only remember a few experiences with him. I wanted to do it differently. I wanted to be there for my family and experience the development of my children firsthand. I wanted to take time whenever necessary for my family. And I wanted to make money with meaningful work. I wanted to be of benefit and enjoy using my time and skills in a good way.

Soon I began my first project: I traveled the world on my own. When I was 19 years old I made a trip around the world. Many more long-distance journeys were soon to follow. When I was 23 years old, I made an experience that left a deep mark:

Madagascar, August 1994:

My flight home is completely overbooked. The next plane supposedly departs in four days. Because of that, Air Madagascar pays a stay in the Hilton hotel. I am still studying at university – on top of that, I had just traveled through the country with my backpack for five weeks – so the unexpected stay in a luxurious hotel is perfect.

While the marble bathtub is filling with water and I am looking forward to washing myself after all these weeks, I look down to the streets from the 18th floor. Huts made of wood and metal sheets are standing side by side. The street lighting makes everything look pale and green. Women are cooking on small, open fireplaces. Children in ragged clothes and sooty black faces are playing football. They use tin cans and plastic bottles as balls.

Those are kids who fish leftovers from the small restaurants' plates before they are thrown away. Children who express utmost joy if they receive a bread roll or some cookies.

Questions are coming up in my head:

> Why am I, at age 23, up here and not down there like so many others?

> Why do these impressions affect me so much?

> How can I use my skills and opportunities to support others while at the same time enjoy myself and earn an income for a perfect life?

Right after I graduated in construction engineering, I founded a construction management company. The challenges were big and during this phase, I lost track of my goals because of stress, time pressure, tension and responsibility. They were covered by the daily "fight for survival" and would only come back to light about ten years later.

This "fight" developed through the assumption that I would have to interact "decently" and "like an adult" and that I was supposed to take responsibilities. I wanted to have an income, to be able to take care of my family later. The ambition to raise a company from nothing into success was a huge burden on me. At one point or another, it always pushed me down to the ground.

I was afraid to turn my hobby into my profession and to make a living out of photographs and slideshows. Even though this path has been so easy for me so far and it indeed showed some success, I didn't take the next step. It was just not "real work". I turned away from my path and ignored my feelings, just to take the allegedly safer path.

With the backpacking trips on all continents I wanted to do something nobody else in my circle of friends had ever done before. The fears of my family and friends made me feel insecure. How did they want to judge a journey if they had never undertaken one themselves? Next to my training and university, I earned enough money to afford the flight tickets, equipment and plenty of specialised literature. I didn't need more. I realized my plans. I admit I was a little bit naive sometimes, yet always successful.

Regarding my career choice, I did not have that much courage. Family, friends and acquaintances were suddenly superior with their experiences. Each of my acquaintances worked a bourgeois job and everyone of them – from an external point of view – seemed to do fine. Because of that, I decided for the building industry, a down-to-earth and allegedly future-proof industry. I still took the step of becoming self-employed, but not on the photography and speech path. **I was too afraid to follow my feelings and choose my own path.**

The "down-to-ground" plan was the following: My company was supposed to secure me financially so that I would not have to rely on the daily income. Then I could take some time – I thought so – for my visions and goals. However, despite a lot of commitment and many working hours, I did not fully reach my goal with this plan.

At the age of 38 I had a nice house already, but financially seen I did not yet have the desired scope. Because of the burden, I was also frustrated, stressed and often sick. I felt like my life was just passing by.

Out of this situation, I developed a process of self-discovery which I initially underestimated. The more I dealt with it, the more questions were raised:

> Why am I still often in bad mood, despite my professional "success"?

> Why do I allow the stress to make me sick?

> How is this supposed to work later on when I also have children?

At first, I couldn't find any answers to those questions. I only knew that I didn't want to be a discontented and irritable father to my children. For the children of the world I hadn't done much so far either.

In seminars for personal development and in books – from meditation to project management – i found many answers.

But the amount of detailed information every now and then drove me to the brink of despair. Furthermore, there are apparently countless possibilities on how to interpret, filter and combine those advices. The practical application, as well as the combination with other aspects of my life raised problems.

Matters were made worse by the fact that this radical change for me – as well as for many others – happened in a phase of my life in which I already had way too much to do anyway. It required a lot of commitment to financially make ends meet with a wife, three children and a house.

But in the end, the most important thing is to combine creativity and success. To find your own path, free and independent. Or should I say: to rediscover your path? It is important to be determined. To live exactly that life of your imaginations. To have time for yourself and for the people you love. To use a system that will lead you to more time, more money and more joy.

Do you want it too?

This book can help you find answers to the following questions quickly and efficiently:

> How can we permanently bring more time, more money and more joy into our lives?

> How can we be sure that the path we are taking is really ours?

> How do we withstand the internal and external pressure of "being different"?

> What is the result of the changes we make?

> What are the reasons that let us keep up?

> Where do we put our fears and doubts?

> Where do we find the energy to reach our goals?

> When will we actually be successful?

> How do we stay successful?

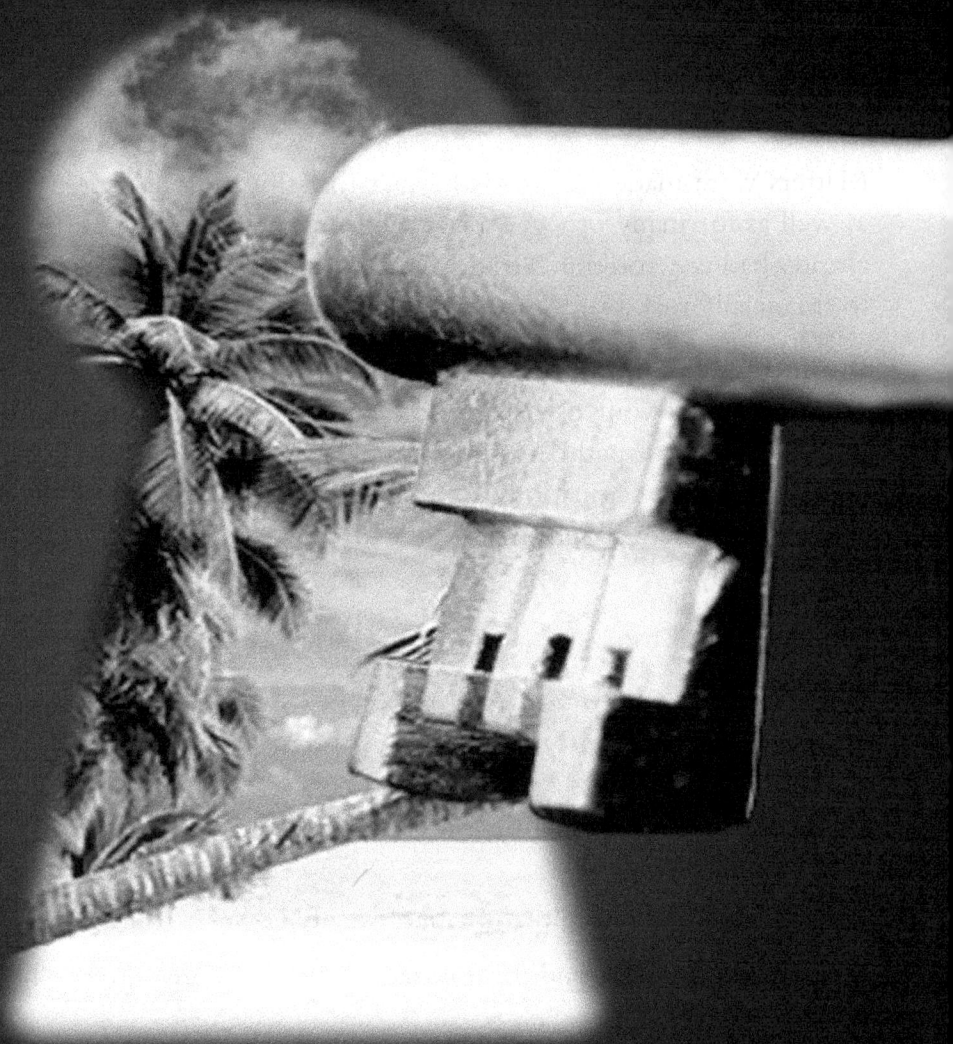

KEY 1

FROM THE STRESS TO THE DREAM

A wonderful life

If you want to build a house, you have to know what **you** like. You also have to decide what amount of money you want to invest in your house. A good architect can then make valuable suggestions for the design, planning and execution. But he will never be able to say what **your** dream house has to look like.

The purpose of this book is to give you some different perspectives and ideas for design, planning and execution of your life. This way, you will have much energy left to reach your goals and live a wonderful life. At the same time, the book will help you minimize your power loss.

Not all of those "wisdoms" and methods are coming from me as I am not demanding to reinvent the wheel. With "Engineered Success – Turn your Vision into Profit", I have put synergy into realizations from Anthony Robbins, Bruce Lipton, Deepak Chopra, Frank Kern, JT Foxx and many others as well as historical sources. ONE system developed from those, which will simply and efficiently lead to more success in the professional and private everyday life.

From the perspective of an entrepreneur and engineer, I only picked those subjects that proved successful and are crucial according to my own experience. With this book, you are holding a strategy in your hands that will help you step by step to create the life you are dreaming of – or used to dream of.

Every permanent success develops through synergies

Stress – its forms and effects

Stress is a common term and is often used when we don't know which way to turn. We sometimes either don't finish tasks at all, too late or unfocused and slide from one catastrophe to the next. Soon enough we are completely exhausted.

Stress is a mental and physical reaction caused by external stimulants. We make a distinction between Eustress which is useful in certain situations and drives us to achieve outstanding results and distress. The last mentioned is the long lasting, strong stress from which we suffer.

From science we know that our body produces specific substances in stress phases which will last until the stress stops – the danger, is over. The body is doing that because it wants to fight the threat by all available means. Historically speaking: "Run away from the lion or fight it!"

Both options require an incredible amount of energy which will be made available by the body in this moment. A "turbo boost" of the body. What we can easily comprehend is the fact that this "turbo boost" does not last forever. Quite literally, it leads to a "burnout" of the boost, because the body can't deliver the additionally required energy forever without taking damage.

I think this is quite logical. Even though I was not aware of the necessary steps the body takes in order to produce so much available energy within a fraction of a second and to maintain it, sometimes for a long period of time.

Which consequences do we have to expect when we are facing permanent stress? It doesn't mean more than the fact that our body is constantly producing energy ahead of its performance limit. Where is it taking this energy from? It doesn't produce power at the moment it is required but instead, it metaphorically short circuits other systems for a short period of time – or even for a long period of time.

Bruce Lipton, a US American development biologist and stem cell researcher addresses the first resource for the lasting maintenance of the stress level, the shut down of the supply of the digestive system as well as the reduction of the cell regeneration of organs.

Each cell in our body dies at some point in our life and will be replaced by a new one. This is a constant process. We only notice it when we injured ourselves and the wound is magically healing by itself. All organs, bones etc. will be consistently renewed and redeveloped without us noticing. For a certain period of time, we can pause or heavily reduce this process without noticing. However, in the long run, we age faster and some aspects prematurely lose their functions. We then tend to blame our age and comfort ourselves with the fact that everyone has some issues here and there.

Just imagine what would happen if we would never check our car for maintenance? Sooner or later a damage will occur which would have occurred much later if we had taken care of the car.

But that's not just it. The next system our body is taking energy from, for the occurrence and the maintenance of is the immune system, which protects us internally and externally from infections. When we are healthy, we hardly notice how much energy our protection systems require. We will realize this once our body is not healthy anymore. If we are lying in bed with a flu and are not able to do anything at all. Neither physically, nor mentally. The immune system then works at full blast and hardly leaves any energy to other systems itself. Have you ever been completely stressed while having a flu and could manage to find any energy left?

While transplanting an organ, the patient will receive a treatment with stress hormones so that the immune system will be weakened and does not have the energy to fight the new and foreign organ as an "intruder".

With those examples, I realized that a constantly high level of stress is making us very vulnerable. We lower our defense and charge forward with everything we have. If we are a little bit behind in a final match shortly before the final whistle, this might lead to a success, but nobody will win the world championship like this.

Stress can secure the survival, but it can also spoil it for us.

What matters to us are the questions:

❯   What is getting us into this condition of permanent stress?

❯   How can we get out of this condition again?

Why are we stressed?

If we don't have any clear and mandatory goals, we are very affected by distractions. Those distractions require a lot of energy and time. But we need both, in order to complete our tasks well and in time. If we waste too much time, it will be missing in other spots. This will create a vicious cycle.

Here, the question is raised: What does distractions mean? Someone who is distracted, allows people and circumstances to take too much control. In the end, we are controlled by anything that happens around us. How much depends on each person individually.

It can be very trivial things that have an impact on us. A cluttered working space, a screen frame covered in sticky notes or opened folders spread across the office that are always making us feel like we haven't finished a task yet.

The least we know our goals, the worse we can focus on what we need to achieve our goals. This makes us very receptive for recommendations and distractions.

The consequences are obvious:

If we are not working focused on one thing, we will not finish within the desired timeframe and in the required quality. At the same time, a lot of other tasks accumulate which then hang like a sword of Damocles above our heads. A pressure situation develops. We don't feel comfortable anymore, fear grows continually. If we now receive fitting criticism from family, the supervisor or the customer, our trust and confidence will be deprived. We lose the ground below our feet. Fear turns into stress.

We are stressed because we are scared:

> Scared of not being able to finish all these tasks in the budgeted time

> Scared of doing something wrong

> Scared to miss something important

> Scared of not being able to overcome something unknown or a change

Stress is very closely connected to the fear of not reaching goals in the estimated time and quality. Therefore, stress, fear, time, quality, and goals are connected to each other.

Distance and Overview

I am very glad that you – despite the stress, lack of time and maybe so many fears still managed to read this book so far. You have taken the first step already, you took a couple of minutes and managed to distance yourself for a while from the events in the day. A lot of people already fail to do so.

The next challenge is to take time for planning. We do that very rarely and react spontaneously in the situation instead of getting an overview first in order to be able to act planned and structured. We just start somewhere and let ourselves get pulled into the whirl of the everyday life that repeats itself for years and often leads to unsatisfying results.

What would happen:

> If we had enough time to fully think through all of our tasks, to plan them and then completing them in peace?

> If we could be confident that everything is going to work and the above-mentioned fears are completely unreasonable?

> Most of us would take a deep breath, relax and start the day with joy and optimism. We would experience the day consciously and the results would pile up.

It is important to create free spaces to give ourselves room for development. So we should first of all search for these free spaces and then use them in order to create the life we are dreaming of. With the help of our abilities and knowledge.

The fears will dissolve little by little or at least reduce significantly while you are finding out through this book, which keys you need for personal success and how to use them in the correct order.

Let us create free spaces first, in order to evolve. A few hours per week should be enough for the start.

Where is our valuable time?

But what do we do with our time? The time we need for tasks in our professional and private life?

Let's take the news as an example: We can't do much about a civil war in Africa. We also don't have the intention to go to a demonstration or to commit ourselves to the cause in other ways. And yet we invest so much time in those complex subjects. We are watching the daily news and read several newspaper articles.

Another example is the weather. It is interesting to know what the weather will be like from Monday to Friday. But in order to pick the right clothes in the morning on our way to the office, a glance out of the window would be enough already.

If those examples do not apply to you, you will very likely find other areas which may not be vital for you but which you still dedicate a certain amount of time to. We invest a lot of time in order to be informed about things that may not even affect us, that we are not even interested in. There is something new going on every single day – and in the end, nothing actually changes. Therefore we are wasting precious lifetime just to feel pressured in a different area, so much that we even get sick because of that.

Often, this useless information puts us into a state of fear, unease or anger. They sometimes make us feel guilty.

I do not want to claim that news are unimportant. But we should ask ourselves how often we want to deal with them and what significance they have in our lives.

My key experience was the Middle East conflict. After the death of my grandparents, I decluttered an old cupboard in the garage. My grandmother had laid out the cupboards with newspapers. When I cleaned up, I took out one of these papers and read the headline. "Middle East conflict escalated" it said in some antiquated writing. An hour before I had read the same headline, only in modern letters. It was in our current daily newspaper. I read the old report. The only difference between the "garage report" from 1965 and the current report from the year 2002: the names of the actors had changed.

Up to this point, I had dealt extensively with the Middle East conflict. I spent a lot of time in reading and discussing. I had illuminated the backgrounds and forged plans for solutions. And now I had to realize that most of my "findings" already appeared in the article of 1965, a report written before my birth.

At that moment, I decided to drastically reduce my consumption of daily news and to read only once a week. Interestingly, I still receive all the information that are important. And without the daily hassle of about an hour!

My knowledge is always enough for talking. If something really interests me, then usually one or two qualified reports suffice to adapt to additional background knowledge. This is much more fundamental than anything I could convey to the daily, superficial reports.

Take the time to define your own future!

As a thinking game I would like to add the following calculation: If we had saved one hour per day since 2005, that would be 365 hours times 12 years. That is 4,380 hours, so 182,5 days. In other words: We would have saved half a year of a lifetime! Incredible, isn't it?

1 hour x 365 days x 12 years = 1 half of a year of a lifetime. How many hours per day to you invest in your consumption of news?

> *Consider for yourself how much time you spend every day just to be "informed". Are there not any more important things in your life that you could do in t his time?*

Don't worry, we will find many other places where you can save time if the news doesn't work. But try it yourself: invest a few minutes each day to not listen to the news and instead read this book. **Give yourself the freedom to discover your visions, and take the time to determine your future**. Then you will notice how your stress level falls and that more phases of relaxation are entering your life.

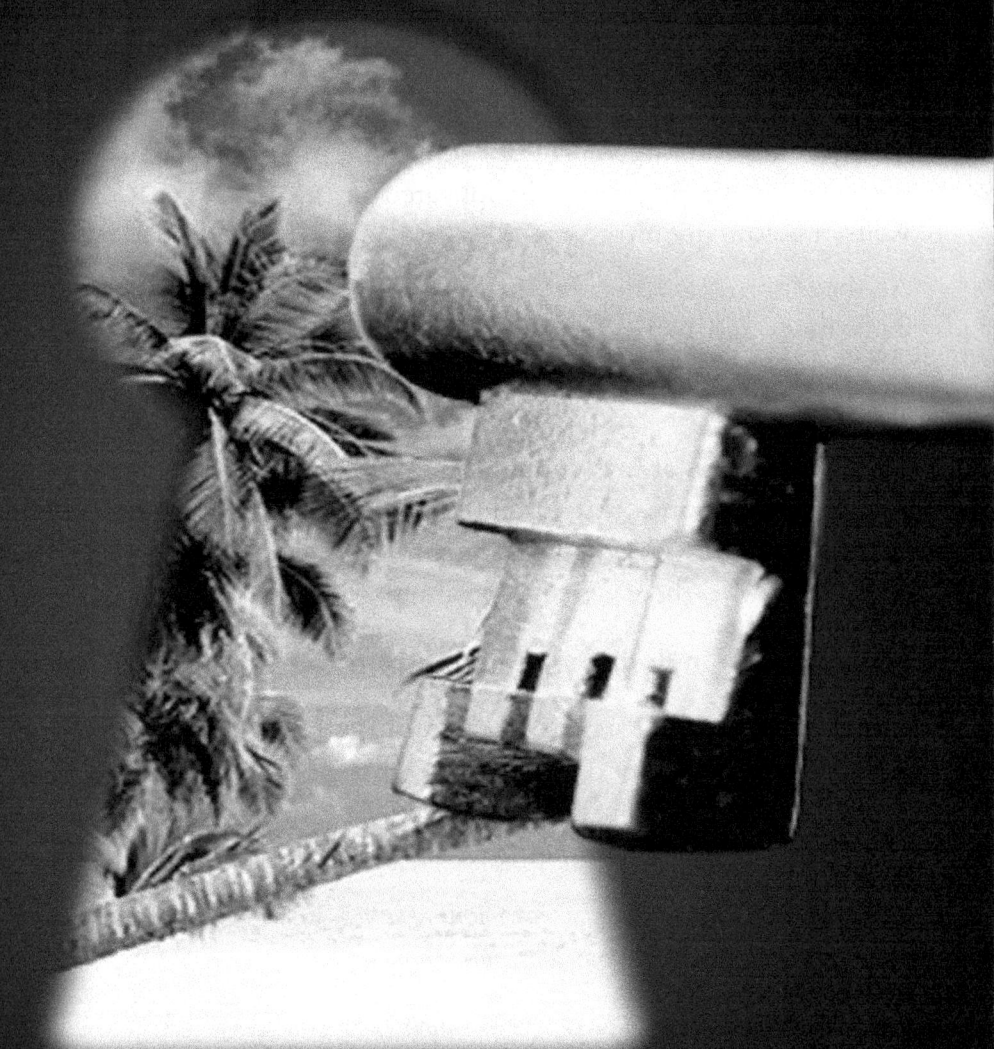

KEY 2

GIVE YOUR VISIONS AND GOALS ROOM TO DEVELOP

Visions are visual images of our future. They do not include a specific plan. They are thoughts, ideas, dreams, in which we imagine what our lives should look like in 5, 10, 20 or 30 years and what we want to achieve by then.

Many people have not thought about those things all too much. It requires strength to deal creatively with one's life dreams. After a busy day, it is often difficult to get up again. If, for example, the children have to go to bed, the evening is quickly over again. And soon afterwards also the week, the month, the year ... Our visions are forgotten. This is a pity because:

With visions we determine our lives in advance.

Visions create facts

Taking time for your own visions – this is the first step out of your everyday life. You will always find a few minutes to do so. If not, then leave out watching the late night news.

Listen to relaxing music. Let yourself drift away. Close your eyes and dream your wildest future dreams. No matter what happens. Enjoy your stay in your future. Imagine your family. What does your future family look like? How did your children develop? What trips do you want to make, which concerts do you want to visit? What will you be able to do? Who will you meet? Where do you live? What does your house look like? What have you accomplished professionally, what is your dream job? Do you work in your dream job? Indulge and let yourself feel good. After 10–15 minutes you come back to the present. Stretch and breathe deeply. You are back in the present. Unfortunately, none of your visions have become reality yet. Stay tuned, it will happen. Sure, you have sometimes dreamed of your future like this. But what happens after the return to the present? Soon you will be back in your everyday life, and all your worries, your needs and the lack of time push your visions into the background. Let us take another path here! A path that leads you step by step from your visions to the realization. You already brought a lot with you that you are going to need for this path.

There is probably a map missing, which gives you an orientation. Only with this map you can check your route and correct it if necessary. If the necessary energy is added, you will be successful on your way.

> *The phase in which you are building your vision is decisive for future success or failure.*

The clear vision is essentially responsible for whether we experience "flow" or frustration. It is the idea-finding, the basis for the design-planning. If this foundation stone is not stable, you can still make corrections in the further expansion phases only with extreme effort.

Visions become tangible goals

Visions, simply said, are dreams, desires, distant ideas. But they are also the foundation and the driving force for a happy and successful life. We dream about the desired final state and feel comfortable.

> *"Our desires are pre-emotions of the abilities that lie within us, precursors of what we can accomplish. What we can and would do is to imagine our imagination apart from us and in the future; We feel a longing for what we already have in our lives. Thus a passionate anticipation transforms the truly possible into a dreamed reality."* - Goethe

Goals are the continuation of our visions into reality. There are final goals and intermediate goals, great goals and small ones. For visions to become reality, we must set goals for ourselves and try to achieve them. They are, so to speak, the building blocks for the vision. The clearer the vision, the better we can derive the objectives from it. Clear objectives allow for a clear approach.

> *Finding a goal is a process, not a one-time event.*

An example for the power of concrete goals

In a study by the University of Yale, the students of the final year were asked whether they had a plan for their future lives and whether this was written down. The very least had such a written plan. Twenty years later, the still living graduates were asked again. Among other things, they were asked about their lifestyle, their contentment and their wealth.

Interestingly, just the few who had formulated a plan were mostly living an upscale lifestyle and experienced great satisfaction. The real conviction, however, was that this tiny group had more financial resources than all the others together.

Goals are often superimposed on beliefs

When was the last time you listened to your inner voice? Listened to the lad or the lass deep inside of you? Perceived him or her pounding on the door somewhere in the subconsciousness? How they want to get out, laugh and dance? Why do we leave the inner child so little space to unfold? I wonder where I lost the contact. When did life become so "serious" that I had no time for pranks? Or were the fears so severe that I buried my plans again?

Growing up means taking responsibility. "You're already big now." "You have to earn some money." "What will you become one day?" "What do the others think?" These sayings should be familiar to some of us.

It creates enormous pressure, but usually without any solutions or instructions. Without a guide with which we could find out what we really want. Even if we have managed to inform ourselves in detail about the professional goals we have, our own views and our environment are constantly changing. It is very difficult to change the decision once made for a certain profession

We take responsibility, not only for ourselves, but also for our partner and our children, for our parents or other close people. When a parent dies or is not there anymore because of a divorce, children often take wide responsibilities. Without realizing it, they are distracted by themselves and are moving further and further away from their own life goals.

The inner child, our feeling, is quickly submerged and is never seen again in most people. Except in certain areas, where these people then show very extreme behavioral patterns to compensate for what is suppressed elsewhere. The oppressed feeling has yet another possibility to gain attention, namely by making the body and the spirit sick.

To be able to laugh of joy once again, consciously listening to our own feelings, and trusting them, is the art we need to learn to discover. This is also of crucial importance in the goal identifying process. We should not suppress the inner voice reflexively, and we should not dismiss the incipient thoughts as crazy. It has already been the reason why many desires and longings are rising. Even those who are embarrassing to me as an adult. - Are they really embarrassing? Or wouldn't it be wonderful to sometimes"just allow ourselves to do" certain things just? But we wouldn't dare. What would the others think? What if it doesn't work? ...

These patterns often hamper the process of goal finding. They act as filters and nip our dreams in the bud.

Many people categorically exclude any possibility of extra-service and more leisure. Because they basically think: "Nothing comes from nothing." And this thought process continues: "Only if you work more, you can get more money out of it."

Clearly speaking, this means: I am working 15 hours per week more and therefore earn accordingly more. They think it is unrealistic to have more time.

But there are also people on this planet who are working the same amount as I do but earn a lot more than me. "Well, they are better educated than me.", I would think immediately. But that is very often not actually the case.

There are even people who are educated much worse than we are, who surely didn't worry as much about their lives as we did – and they still earn more money and spend less time in the office than we do. It's especially frustrating for us if those people, on top of that, are also happy in their lives.

Let us, therefore, create the space and the freedom for every goal that comes to our mind.

In which mood do we define our goals?

Often we are not in the best mood while searching for our goals.

If I start my day stressed and try to figure out where to start, then this isn't a good prerequisite to imagine our future in bright colours.

Many, however, do not tackle their goal until there are already problems occurring. If we feel like we slowly have to start doing something, then everything is still alright. However, if the pressure is already so strong that we are forced to act, it is already a great challenge to find peace and time in order to deliberately deal with our own goals.

I HAVE to do something – the choice of words already shows that we don't really like doing something. The motivation, the enthusiasm is not to be found. And this is not the ideal prerequisite for a visionary day dream.

We don't believe in our great goals

Here, a process starts which I didn't understand for a long time. I have to make my subconscious mind understand that we can achieve anything, as soon as we pull together. We, that is my mind, my thoughts, my feelings, my subconsciousness.

If I don't feel confident enough to do something, nobody else will believe in my success. These doubts lead to not achieving my goals.

I can't sell my product very well if I am not convinced by its usability. The product, in this case, are my experiences, ideas and goals. I myself am the buyer. Therefore, I can only "sell" my goals to myself if I really believe in them.

To start believing in our own goals, it is necessary to build up on small goals and achievements. We have to be aware of our achievements. Because it may happen that we reach goals and make achievements without noticing it. We only see the issues we have and forget about what we have done already.

Write down your answers to these questions in key points:

> What should be the result of my work in five minutes?

> What is the desired goal of the next meeting?

> Which are the most important goals for this week?

Do write down your goals. Check the points you have already achieved. Start right now: write down a few points that you can easily realize today, tomorrow or until the end of the week.

If you have reached them, set a thick, green tick behind it and be happy about it. This way, you can show your consciousness and your subconscious that achieving goals is normal and something positive for you.

Every reached goal is a feeling of success. It is a pleasure. And things that bring pleasure want to be experienced over and over again.

Goals like: "I will go out for dinner with my wife once a month" or "I will meditate twice per week" are easy to implement. In a relaxed atmosphere, we come up with new ideas. Or we just have fun and enjoy the evening. We can also be proud of that. And we should look forward to it because success is based on success. Mountain climbers already know this phenomenon: After the first four thousand meters high mountain, there follows a five thousand meters high one. It is a matter of one's own demands and expectation. Turn the joint meal or the monthly visit to the cinema with a dear person to your success experience. You have "choked" the time elsewhere, so you have managed to stop yourself from watching TV every evening and started a creative alternative program instead.

Because of these successes with smaller goals, your self-confidence will soon start believing that you can also achieve big goals. This whole strategy is developing dynamics and you soon will want more: there are no limits, everything is achievable.

Build a foundation made of successes!

It does not necessarily have to be set and achieved goals. In order to build up a stable foundation of positive events, many things can serve you.

How do we manage to gather and save many smaller and bigger achievements? And how do we make ourselves aware of them? Just think about all the good things you have done and experienced in the past years!

Start noting down all the positive memories of your childhood, your teenage years, your professional and private life. Take a walk and indulge in reminiscences about the happiest and most exciting moments. Take a smartphone or a dictating machine with you and record your experiences in key points. Access every part of your life: romantic moments, decisions that you are proud of, etc. Everything is allowed, whether they are first steps or revolutionary deeds. What matters is that it is a success in your opinion. Think about the concerts you visited or books that gave you decisive impulses.

When did you laugh wholeheartedly? When were you completely impressed? Full of excitement? When did you help someone a lot? Feel and enjoy the pride you felt in these moments! In which moment were you incredibly grateful? Who did you hug? Who hugged you?

Think about the day that has passed or the last week. Note down the great moments you had.

Keep the list safely so you can access it at any time.

Now you have the first list of positive events that you can watch or listen to again and again. Your experiences won't disappear somewhere in the past any longer but are available at any time. Add more and more to your collection! Write down the best events on a weekly basis and mark them with a text marker! This is how you find good impulses from your own life when "the roof falls on your head". The longer the list, the more you will be convinced of yourself. You will believe that you achieve your goals. Even such goals, which appear to be unrealistic.

Because now you have activated your consciousness and reminded it of what you have already achieved. It is quite clear: you want more of it. Your subconscious will also believe more and more. It will do everything to help you achieve your goals.

At this point, I would like to recommend you write down all the important thoughts that come up while reading this book in a notebook. Choose something elegant, because your life is worth to be documented in an elegant setting! It is a nice feeling to write in such a book and to read it from time to time. Find your own system, but please keep in mind that what is written in a solid book will stay there for a long time. Let's call it the "book of life."

Great memories will help you design your future in a positive way.

Clearing your mind with exercise

Similar to diamonds hidden in the rocks, many important goals lie deep inside us. How do we approach them when they are covered by our everyday life?

In order to develop our goals with joy and imagination, we must first free ourselves from the current pressure situation. May it be through sport or through a hobby, there is always something that can guide our circular thoughts in a new direction.

Often, I get the best ideas and pictures while walking in the forest. It starts after about twenty minutes when I slowly change to "walking automatically". The trees move past me, I get into a kind of meditative state, which suppresses my everyday worries and gives rise to joy. The joy to run as fast as I like. Pleasant thoughts rise from this joy.

With increasing physical exertion, the point of view almost always shifts. Where there was still an impenetrable thicket of problems, solutions are suddenly emerging. Often, I run with a dictation machine, to be able to record my thoughts as soon as they arise.

Now the process is really going on. After the "worries" were treated while running, I feel a great relief, a great happiness. This leads me to run too fast. The pulse counter is crazy, and I feel freer, the faster I run. After a few kilometers, my running speed settles down again due to condition deficits, and the ideas are just flowing towards me. A so-called "flow state" emerges, in which everything appears feasible, in which the boundaries disappear and we feel comfortable. The trees, the birds, the whole nature and I, we are in harmony. This is an incredible force.

This is the state in which I develop my visions and keep my goals. Here in the forest, my reasons become more conscious, my emotions clearer. A variety of thoughts and ideas are stored on my dictation machine, lined with a loud breath. When showering, the thoughts refine to correct strategies. I write them down at the same point, in order to not lose any thought or context. Writing down is very important because thoughts come and go. I've spent a lot of time trying to reconstruct forgotten thoughts. And only rarely has it succeeded completely.

What I achieve while walking, others do when cycling, mountaineering, walking, playing golf, whatever it is. It is important to get out of the everyday life, to dive into its own world and to think and feel beyond the previous limits. Just do it!

Find your own way to get into this state! Even meditation can be helpful. In my experience, however, it is most likely to work well when the body is exhausted and the problem-thinking has been put to its limits. Relaxing, releasing tension, concentrating on something quite different, e.g. Running may be an essential point.

It is often only about overcoming the inner weakness, and to do something when it's raining outside, too. However, I know from my own experience: the shower after a run in bad weather is even finer. And it is wonderful to arrange the thoughts with the tea cup in your hand and to write the discovered goals cleanly into your book. This is also a success.

Physically, you can do a lot to think more freely
and more courageous.

Visualising the success and enjoying it in advance

Philipp Lahm said in an interview that he had looked at the victory of the 1990 World Cup again and again. In 1990, he was six years old. He had so often dreamed about it, Lahm said, that he had almost become one with this image.

Goalkeeper Sepp Maier gave the same answer when he was asked in 1974 whether it was exciting, to stand up there, with the World Cup in his hands. He said roughly: "It was a familiar feeling, I had visualized and imagined it so often since my childhood".

If we were aware of how much effort is required to become a successful football player, we would probably find it hard to be ready to start the game with full enthusiasm. The thoughts of pain and deprivation would be too great, the ever-present temptations to give up, too strong. Only those who can feel the joy and appreciation that will come with the achievement of the goal IN ADVANCE will have the strength to withstand.

Visualize the desired final state as detailed as possible. Pretend like it is already reality!

Collages – Energy in word and image

Future collages are pictures of our goals, glued to a large, colored paper, combined with energized sentences. They help us to recall the feeling described above. We can orient ourselves on the pictures and they help us remember the right feeling. Better yet, we put our minds into our cabrio and feel the warm wind blowing around our ears, we hear the motor roar...

In many seminars, I understood the idea behind collages in a way that it is enough to stick a few colorful pictures onto a piece of paper and look at the work again and again. In the course of time, however, I had to realize that things were not as fulfilling as I would have liked. Although I had a lot of trouble with the selection of photos and texts. But somehow this worked quite well in some areas, but in other areas, not even a bit.

I came to the conclusion that collages are in principle an excellent support module. However, they only fulfill their purpose when I deeply believe in the future I represent. If the pictures really fit me and I feel an inner joy while looking at the collage. Again, it is about the feeling that arises when I look at the "tool" pictures.

Before we go into the details, you will find your goals and begin to implement them, I would like to give you an example. It shows how things can develop, even if you do not know every detail at the beginning and only have a rough planning from the travel route. What can happen when you just get started, get involved in life and travel a little further each day. Things happen, which you do not know at the beginning, that they exist at all. How could I have dreamed of it?

In addition, you will suddenly be perceived differently by people who were more than skeptical before. What seemed impossible yesterday, while there were countless (sometimes justified) objections, is normal today. It is even supported and imitated.

Just start!

At the beginning of the 1990s, it was not as usual to fly around the world for a few months as a 19-year-old. If I had known before the beginning of my world trip what I knew after another 10 individual trips, I would probably never have left. At least not in such a completely carefree mood. At that time, nothing really bad happened to me. Only positive experiences.

Unexpectedly, as an example, I find myself alone standing in the dark on top of the Uluru and see the sun rise over Australia (today I would no longer go up there, out of respect for the beliefs of the Aborigines, but back then, I didn't know so many things). I had seen this monolith as a little boy in a book, and I knew I would go there one day. Because at that time I had no idea of the distance and the costs, for my subconsciousness it was simply a clear announcement, that I would reach one day.

In Hawaii, I experienced a small lava eruption. I later received 1,000 DM for the photos of it.

After this successful start, there was nothing to prevent further journeys. I believed that I would manage them well, and my environment shared this opinion. "He will be fine," was now said from all sides. It did not matter if it was Greenland or Madagascar on the roadmap. In addition, I suddenly had a certain reputation as a photographer, though – apart from the manual of my camera – I hadn't read anything about photography. It was a curiosity and unconstrained, relaxed action which had opened up many new possibilities for me.

Through curiosity and unbiased, relaxed actions, a cycle of success had developed and opened up many new possibilities for me.

> *Cycles of success often seem like a „lucky coincidence".*
> *But they are based on patterns that we use consciously*
> *and implement them into our everyday life.*

Let's make it concrete: You have already documented positive experiences in your book. You are aware of your foundation. This is decisive in order to be able to believe in your potential. But how do you find the visionary goals that fit you, now?

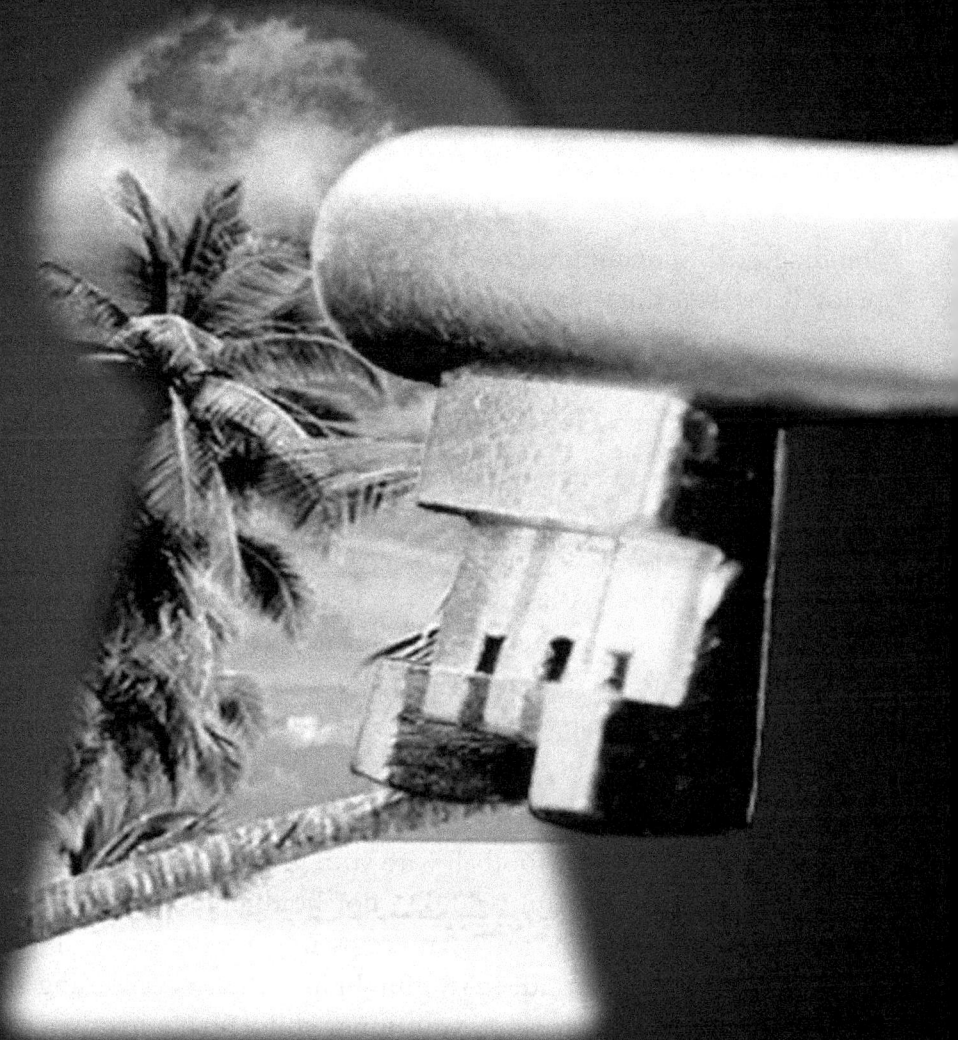

KEY 3

LISTEN TO YOUR INNER VOICE TO FIND YOUR REAL GOALS

„It is not a shame to not reach your goals, but it is a shame to not have any goals" Viktor Frankl

Finding goals, pursuing them despite distractions and achieving them is a joy. It gives us the strength to continue to grow and unfold. Everything around us also grows and thrives better when we are a source of joy, success, and gratitude. How does this work? I admit it requires some discipline and work. How to do it is summarized here in a few steps.

Get yourself into an energetic state! How? – Through sport, dance, music … Stand up and stretch yourself. Stretch to the left and right sides. Inhale and exhale deeply a few times. Now write down every personal goal that comes to your mind! What would you like to achieve in 20 years? At the moment, it does not matter if you want to start it right now or only in a few years. Write for 5 minutes as fast as you can. Try not to think, but just write. Do not write it down in details. But stay specific so you have a picture. It's enough if you know later what you meant. "Porsche 911 in silver" is enough. What equipment it should have stays in your mind.

Perhaps you want to play football with your grandchildren? It is important to let the imagination run wild. Do not hold anything back. Ignore all boundaries and write down what "pops up in your head". No matter how absurd it may sound. It is your brainstorming according to your goals. Here your subconscious, your inner child, finally has the chance to be heard. You can still erase things later.

Personal goals

What personal goals do you have for the next 20 years?

Examples of my goals:

> Traveling to the USA and flying through the Grand Canyon with a helicopter

> Writing books about things that are important, and give lectures about it

> Going on a cultural journey once a year with my wife

> Living in a really good hotel for skiing holidays with the family once a year

> Having enough time and money to travel the world with my family in the school holidays

> Learning Spanish

> Traveling on a research ship to the Antarctica with my family

> Listening to the best singers of the world in the Sydney Opera House

> Crossing the Alps by foot and by bike

> Learning how to sail and then do regular sailing tours

> Biking through the Alps with my children

> Supporting the environmental protection

> Having no back pain anymore

> Becoming vegetarian and hiring a cook who cooks three times per week for us

> Now write down some goals for the next 20 years. Don't worry if not everything is written on the list yet. It is important to internalize this process and practice it on a regular basis. Like so many things in life, it seems quite cumbersome. But you create clarity for yourself and your subconscious mind – that is the decisive point.

Only if something is clearly recognizable, you can focus on it and finally reach it.

I thought at first, it will be fine if I keep my goals " in the back of my head". However, I have regrettably wasted a lot of time, energy and money. Write things down so that they can serve as a basis for your imagination. Dive into your texts, develop colored images. So that the thoughts can take a form. As we shall see later, our thoughts are crucial to our lives.

Your personal goals are now lying in the form of a colorful and very valuable collection in front of you. What do we do with it now? What distinguishes them from short-lived "New Year's Eve goals"?

On New Year's Eve, we are looking forward to the new year. In most cases, however, spontaneous resolutions, according to the motto "It would be good if ...". We have neither a concrete idea of the necessary steps nor are we really trying to follow these noble goals. Some are forgotten a few days later.

The goals that you have just written down are of a very different kind. They have come from within you. And you will see: the more you repeat the process, the clearer your vision becomes, the more solid your visions will be.

Timeline and prioritization

A new project needs additional space, temporal, spatial and intellectual. Let us, therefore, first put your personal goals into an order.

All at once and immediately - this rarely works. Frequently, we have dreams in which every idea for implementation is missing. That is why it is important to give them a certain period of development. Circumstances and ideas change over time, and things that seem "unthinkable" today are going to be part of our daily lives in five years. Therefore, please set your goals in time! What goals do you want to achieve in 1, 3, 5, 10, 20 years? Do not take more than three minutes for that.

Of course, all of them are important, and I would also like to achieve everything right away. But I can not imagine traveling to the Antarctic in a year with the children on a research vessel. They are still too small, and the fascination for Shackleton has not yet reached them. Here are other things that are closer to me and NOW more important.

Ask yourself the question: What do I want to invest in my goal right now - in terms of time, money and mentality? This question often helps to distinguish the most urgent from the less urgent objectives. If the result is 0, 0, 0, I would not set the goal to one year, but choose a realistic time frame.

Years	Goals
2	Traveling to the USA and flying through the Grand Canyon with a helicopter
1	Writing books about things that are important, and give lectures about it
2	Going on a cultural journey once a year with my wife
2	Living in a really good hotel for skiing holidays with the family once a year
2	Having enough time and to travel the world with my family in the school holidays
3	Learning Spanish
10	Traveling on a research ship to the Antarctica with my family
5	Listening to the best singers of the world in the Sydney Opera House
3	Crossing the Alps by foot and by bike
10	Learning how to sail and then do regular sailing tours
10	Biking through the Alps with my children
1	Supporting the environmental protection
1	Having no back pain anymore
1	Becoming vegetarian and hiring a cook who cooks three times per week for us

Due to the time management, we already have a very good overview of the things that we would like to bring into our lives. When I finished my arrangement, I realized that the dissatisfaction about my current situation had already diminished. I had realized that there was still plenty of time left for many things and I do not have to worry about them. On the basis of this order, I was able to peacefully develop strategies for the realization. And I did not have to worry about some goals at all. It is important that the objectives are listed and time-divided.

If you do not want to prioritize, then you will end up like me with my math exam at university. I started with a task, did not manage to do it immediately, tried another one, while the first one was still spinning in my head and destroying any concentration. The look at the clock or at the still unedited back of the task sheet triggered panic every time.

Action without concentration leads to bad results even with sufficient knowledge

My salvation was, after all, the prioritization of achievable points. I invested two precious minutes into calming myself down and another three in the rapid division of my time into the importance of the tasks. Afterwards, I was not smarter, but calmer. At the last minute, I was able to write the result of the penultimate task and got an acceptable mark.

If I had sorted the tasks according to their importance from the start and the time quota was recognized as sufficient, the result would have been much better.

The advantage of such examinations is, of course, the fact that I can usually compensate for a bad result and, even in the worst case, lose a maximum of one semester. In life, this is also possible, but the effort to compensate for bad results is much higher and at some point in time no longer affordable.

The prioritization of your goals shows you how much time and energy you have to plan for each of them. Having a certain plan and defined goals through the day, through the week, the year and the life, leads with certainty to the better results.

Write down the goals in your "book of life". Mark the ones you have reached with a text marker. This is how you build up a database of success stories and document your own development. Always browse in the book and be proud of yourself!

Do not talk to anyone about it. Your goals don't need to be known by others at this point. These are your secrets, your dreams, your fantasies that you must protect now. Because this is a crucial phase of the whole process, in fact for your entire life.

Professional goals

What do the people we admire do? Are those people who doubt themselves and are trapped in their everyday life? Or those who perform extraordinary achievements in their field? Most of the time, the things they do also bring them great joy. They know what they are doing, and everything seems to be easy.

I took a long time to realize that what is easy for me is also valuable. A painter from my circle of acquaintances says about his pictures: "This is not art to me because I know how to do that." Nevertheless, his paintings are worth something – or just because of that.

For a long time, I tried to get better in the areas that were less important to me.

"Strangely enough," I have never really had much hope. It always cost a great deal of overcoming, and as soon as I slowed down, nothing moved. As if you were driving with a pulled handbrake. When it comes to our future planning, we ignore the burning and smell of the overheated brakes for far too long. We give more and more gas and try to "fight forward". At the same time, we would stop in the street, investigate the cause and fix the damage.

To achieve outstanding performance in areas that are not ours, we will hardly succeed. And if so, we have usually paid far too much for the alleged success. Unfortunately, it is expected in our society. For some reason, we have landed in a particular job, and now we have to "make the most of it". The fewest people before the start of their careers have intensively thought about their abilities and their future career. There were a few practical semesters at best, but this was almost too late. The few have gone through a "school of goal-finding". Many, who have not had this happiness, are now deep in professional constraints and don't know how to free themselves.

So, look for your goals. Look for the ones that really make you happy. Because they are often associated with skills that you are good in already.

Find out what you have always liked to do, and bring it into line with your goals!

> In which areas do you still like to learn today?

> What do you like to deal with every day?

It is often not necessary to change everything. In most cases, small changes are enough and everything looks very different after a short time already.

Think about what you want to achieve and how you can achieve these goals step by step with the given skills, your resources, and your goals.

The "parable of entrusted money"

A wealthy man goes on journeys, for the time of his absence he entrusts his servants with his fortune. One gets five talents, the other two, the third servant one talent. What they do with the money is left to them. After the return, the rich man has the following picture: the first servant has made ten out of five talents, the second from two talents four. The third was afraid to lose everything, and did not work with his talent, he did not use it, but buried it and returned it to his master. The Lord then takes away his talent and gives it to the first servant. Mt 25:15; Correspondingly

When this text was written, "Talent" was a currency. But even if the present-day sense of the word is used, the parable is true. We were given abilities which we should use and expand for our own benefit and for the benefit of others. Benefit and improve what we have, rather than bury it fearfully!

Let us start with the goal finding for your professional goals or for your change wishes! Bring yourself into the process and recharge yourself with energy. Get up, put on some energetic music, stretch, bounce, and dance, inhale deeply and exhale deeply. Let go of everything. All constraints, all fears, everything that burdens you, kick it off right away.

Then sit down and quickly write down everything you can think of. What you would like to do, in which you are good and what you want to have changed. Look at the position in which you would like to be. It does not matter now what the consequences would be, and whether it seems possible at the moment. Just write down everything you can think of without thinking about it.

Take seven minutes for it.

As a suggestion, here are a few of my professional goals:

> Get up full of enthusiasm every day and feel joy and gratitude for what I am doing

> Write books and create audio and video programs on topics that are important to me, and document my life's work

> Hold engaging lectures in front of people who want to make more of their lives

> Show people how they can achieve their goals

> Be surrounded by friendly, honest and enterprising people, friends and business partners alike

> Create products from my work that decouple my time from money earning and at least regularly Xy Euro/month

> Have at least XYZ euro per month income from lectures and coaching sessions

> Work creatively, self-employed, independent, and free

> I can select my orders myself

> Further education through at least four top-class seminars per year

> During the school holidays, no appointments have to be carried out

> Have at least four hours per day time for my family

As with your personal goals, you now have a collection of goals and ideas for your professional life.

Arrange the goals in a chronological order. Write again before each goal, until when you must have reached it finally.

Take three minutes for this. Do not think too much, rely entirely on your feeling. Bring your thoughts to paper and create an order. The first thought is often the right one.

Be careful not to tell your goals to anyone immediately. Because most people can not follow your train of thoughts and do not even know your background. Your ideas, visions, and goals are now small, delicate plantlets. You must still protect and care for them to develop. Only after some time are they so robust that they can withstand the storm and have enough substance to overcome dry periods.

If on the other hand, you talk about your goals too early to someone who does not share your euphoria, this often leads to doubts and frustration.

Of course, it is important to get the opinion of others. But only when the reflections have taken on a little more form. Only then will they withstand stress and critical issues. This prevents you from feeling too much insecurity or even being thrown off the track.

Financial goals

Obviously, financial objectives are, in a sense, linked to the professional goals. It is, however, important to consider different investment forms and life stages.

> What secures my income in old age?

> How can I build a financial foundation?

> Where do I invest? In real estate, stocks, gold, silver?

> What hedges do I want to create?

> How can I achieve a basic safety for myself and my family through the yield of my portfolio?

> How would I like to finance my children for their future?

> How much money do I want to have in the pension age or regularly?

Proceed in the same way as with the previous goal-finding processes. Work in an energized state, and leave everything to your pencil on the paper.

Specify your goals

You have now arranged many different goals in a chronological order from three essential parts of your life. From each area, select the two most important goals you want to reach within one year. Write these goals again cleanly on a separate sheet in your "Book of Life". Make the goal more precise than the previous one.

One of my goals could now be for example: We are flying to the USA in summer 2016. For three weeks we tour the West. The main stations are: Grand Canyon, Bryce Canyon, San Francisco and Las Vegas.

For example, if you wrote: "I want to have more vacation," this is quite vague. The goal is already achieved if you take a day more vacation or your boss "gives you one day to compensate for your 200 overtime hours". Of course, you did not mean that. Therefore formulate as exactly as possible.

KEY 4

THE WHY IS IMPORTANT!

*So that you can persistently pursue your goals,
you must not only know what you want. Equally
important is that you know why you want something.*

A sportsman loves the victory. He has a clear picture in his mind, already sees himself on the winner's podium. Recognition, joy, money – all of this is given to him, and from this, he derives a dreamlike life. This is the energy that carries it. That lets him get up when he is lying on the ground. If he had only the tartan track in his head, and the picture of how he would work so hard, round for round, the ambition would be gone soon enough.

*Motivation, ambition, and perseverance are the
results of WHY.*

Many forget to consciously question the WHY and forget to consolidate it with that. But that is the decisive point that pulls us closer to our goals like a magnet. This reason creates all those feelings that are so important for us in reaching the goal.

Imagine you are in the desert. You have no more water, the rescue oasis is several kilometers away. Your energy is dwindling from hour to hour. You want to survive, but this desire to survive is weakened. Exhausted, you sit down in the glowing hot sand. You close your eyes, you don't care for anything anymore.

No, not anything. Suddenly you are thinking about your children. Your children who will grow up without you if you give up now. All at once you can see why you need to go ahead. You will see the future of your children as half-orphans. Deep feelings touch you, and thereby mobilize your last powers.

You see, if you know **why** you want something, you will achieve it

Frequently, however, the reasons are not so clear and not so firmly anchored in our feelings. We have to fix them in writing, or we'll lose them.

The brain can be easily distracted, it learns and is changeable. Therefore, opinions and points of views can change under certain conditions. This can postpone the importance of our goals if they are not set in writing. The exact recording (and of course the frequent reading) is the calibration reference for each goal.

If we now combine emotionally well-fed reasons with precisely defined goals, not even the biggest storms could get us off the track. Even if all the external circumstances have changed and now seem to speak against us.

The WHY of joy (draft)

Write a sentence to each of your one-year goals, about why you need to reach it at any price in that time! How does your life improve when you realize the goal? What joy and benefits do you have, your children, friends, or even strangers? Why can you be proud of it? The text must touch you emotionally. You must feel a joy, a gratitude as if you had already achieved the goal.

Practice this with small examples. Do you remember things you have achieved? Browse through your "Book of Life" and read about your successes. If there are none written down yet, you are now ready to fill the pages.

You can, of course, give up and be annoyed in three years that you did not continue today. Three years of your life have elapsed ...

I certainly do not mean this personally, I speak here of myself as well. I thought too long about it to be able to do without such plans, with the success that the years only slipped through my fingers. Do it better!

As an example my thoughts on the why of joy:

"Only when I write this book can I use my abilities, share my knowledge and inspire myself and others to new things. It inspires me to create a "guide" that contains many of my thoughts, ideas, and experiences and helps those who want to do more with their lives.

My investments in life pay off for me and for others permanently. I am happy to make my findings visible and usable for everyone. I enjoy writing and talking about it."

The WHY of fear (pressure)

Be honest with yourself: imagine what happens if you do not reach the goal. Do you feel really bad when you do not spend the money for your daughter's riding lessons or do not have time to accompany your son to football training? Imagine you are sick and drained in old age because you have not paid any attention to your diet. Your children are most concerned about you. Immerse a few moments emotionally in this scenario.

It is usually easier to build emotions when it comes to impacting others. I speak from personal experience. In the end, everything could not matter to me. I'm going to die. Such an attitude, however, would be copiously and irresponsibly opposed to my family. A coward I would certainly not want to be in this context.

We are afraid of rejection, loss, failure. We do almost everything to avoid such scenarios. Use this energy! Convert brake energy into driving force!

Write a sentence for each of the six-year goals: What happens if I do not reach the goal by the deadline? Have a bit of fear of the consequences. Your subconscious mind will help you avoid the worst case.

Convert brake energy into driving force!

Make your goals visible

Use the following graphic to make your goals visible. It is a wonderful display option, where you can immediately see where you are standing in which area. You can rate your six goals (and two more that are close to your heart) here. How far have you advanced in what areas? I am sure you have already done a great deal of work without being aware of it.

Simply draw a circle on a piece of paper and divide it into 6 or 8 cake pieces. Each cake piece is assigned to a target and is labeled on the outside of the circle segment. The center of the cake is zero. This means that you have not done anything yet, and of course not achieved anything. The circle line stands for 100 percent: here everything is achieved, you are already in the desired state.

Evaluate one of your goals from 0 – 100% and draw a parallel to the edge of the cake at the corresponding value. Repeat for all targets. Then paint the individual pieces of cake in color. You will get a jagged wheel, one that is not yet running smoothly.

So you can immediately see how close you are to the respective goal of your perception. You also recognize how a goal is relative to the others. This, in turn, is important for our subconscious, because it thinks in images. A clearly visible gap would like to close as quickly as possible.

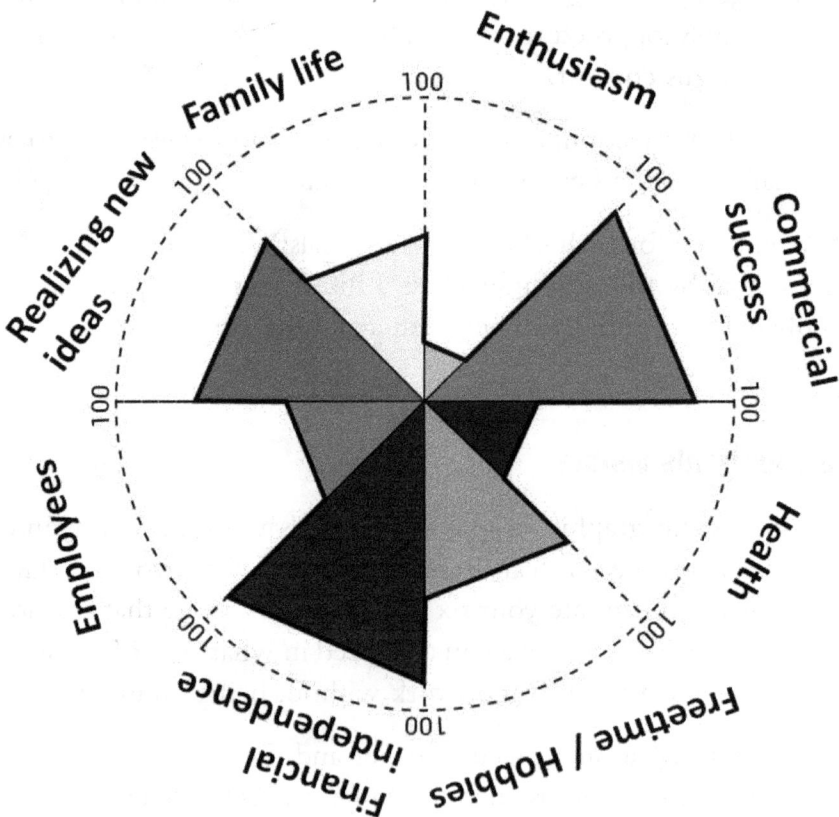

Many people only realize by this description that they have hardly done anything for their private goals, but their professional goals are already at 80 percent or more. In order to let the wheel of life go round, however, all areas are important. Otherwise, the imbalance will destroy the whole wheel when the pressure is too much. And then you have no more joy in the already achieved goals.

The example shows quite general topics. Of course, you can also use this wheel for a single, large target, and divide the necessary steps into cake pieces. Even then you will quickly see the deficits and progress. This gives you a good overview of the project and you know where you should be more active.

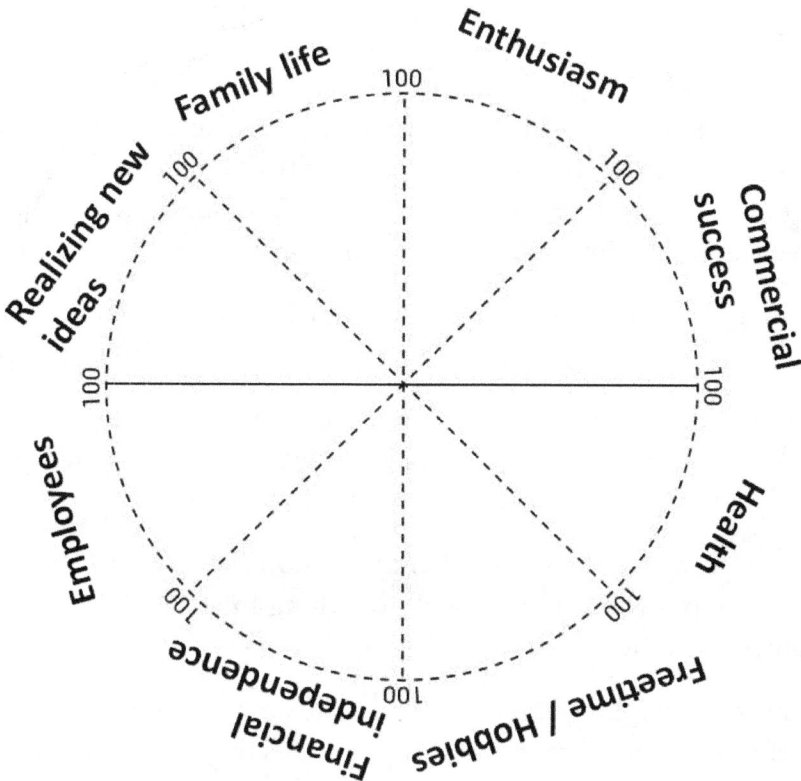

0% is at the center = very bad 100% outside the circle = absolutely outstanding.

Source: Based on Tony Robbin's "Time of Your Life"

Judge yourself, define your current status quo. Can you really accelerate – or is there an imbalance?

You can find the graphic at the following link:

www.christianschwarz.net/buecher/

Looking back from the future

Put yourself in the situation in which you have already achieved all your goals! Imagine you are sitting on your veranda overlooking the sea. You are now 80 years old, the grandchildren play in the garden, while you look back on your life. You think back to the day you wrote down your goals and the reasons. You see the successes, the pleasures, the experiences. You feel a pleasant breeze blowing from the sea. You look forward to every day. You see your wife's relaxed, happy face. You think of all the people you have helped in your life. You feel their gratitude and the warmth of many, many beautiful moments. You are healthy and curious. You radiate joy and happiness, you are one with yourself. The sun slowly goes down. You feel a great gratitude for your life and for what you have created.

Close your eyes for a few minutes. Let your personal pictures rise. Enjoy the look back at your life and feel how joy and warmth spread in you.

Now come back to the present. You are in the here and now. Nothing of what you have dreamed of happened. But you have enough positive reasons and feelings to achieve your goals.

We, however, are so predisposed that we don't only need the pulling power of the positive things to stick to a thing in the long term. No, we sometimes need the so-called

"Kick in the butt". Pressure, anxiety, fears are an essential part of everyday life. And to a certain extent, they are even effective. Fear is an important characteristic. For thousands of years, it warns and protects us from dangers.

If I only think of the compilation of the documentation for the tax declaration, I already feel slightly nauseated. To imagine how relaxed the week between Christmas and New Year will be when everything has already been finished is not enough for me to get it done on time. Just as little as I suppose that I will get money back from the tax office. I will only finish it when I am about to reach the deadline and if I expect the menace of a penalty. Without this pressure, I probably would not have finished the documents. Pressure and anxiety in moderation are often very helpful in order to avoid stress. Build next to your supporting "draft animal" joy the "pusher" pressure up within your imagination.

Your "horror scenario" might look like this: you are 80 years old and see your tired, drained face in the mirror. It's burned out from the life-long struggle for survival. You are divorced. You've been working all your life, always trying to give the best. But there were too many influences that distracted you. You have little contact with your children, the grandchildren you hardly know. In the past, you did not have time to look after your loved ones because of all those "important" things you were busy with. This is how the years go by, day by day, week by week, year by year. Now you no longer need anyone. You are disappointed in life and drink a glass too much every day to distract yourself from your situation. Walking is hard for you. Soon you will need help in your everyday life. Maybe a nursing home? But who is going to pay for it? The stress and the pressure never stop for you ...

How does that feel? How hard are your arms and legs, how big is the pressure? Close your eyes now and make the scene reach into your conscious mind ...

Open your eyes, come back, nothing happened.

You have all the opportunities, all the ways to align your life as you want it to be. You determine your goals.

But keep the pressure in mind. It's going to push you down over the next 40 years if you're not taking care of the really important things in your life. And you have to take care of these things in a way that you and the people around you can get energy out of the process.

Self-check: Do my goals suit me?

Check if it's really your own goals that you've written down there. Ask yourself: Who should I be in order to be the one who achieves these goals? Around which people would I have to be, what clothes should I wear, what should I know, what should I be able to do? Does this really interest me? Or is it just an escape into another situation that I imagine somehow more beautiful than my present one?

Here, a big gap is often created. Because perhaps I don't want to ultimately achieve this goal as I would have to give up or change too many of my qualities as the consequence.

Do you feel comfortable at the thought of your goal, or is there something in your personality that is against it? Think about what you have always been good at. Look further: What have you learned in the past years, which tasks did you do really good?

Write everything down and connect your skills with your goals. Do you manage to fall into a daydream and think about the craziest possibilities at least 10 minutes imaginatively? Are you able to see these ideas and connections as clear ideas before your mind's eye? Do you feel integrated into the scene?

Which people are there in your daydream? Do you feel comfortable in this company or are you insecure? Do you really want to live in this environment, or do you just want to prove something to yourself and others? If everything fits, then you can expect to be on the right track.

Whatever appears in your imagination, be honest with yourself. I've seen a lot of things, but when I was focusing on my feelings intensively, there was usually a slight discomfort in me. Engineer, it's a great job, I can be someone with a name there, I can really have an impact then – that was such an idea. It was clearly influenced by the outside ("You need a clever job!"). I've been through all of this for years.

After all, I ended up with what I've always liked. I like to give lectures and start a movement. To inspire people for a thing or an idea makes me feel great. Especially when the idea is then implemented. In principle, I've already done this as a child, only the themes and the audience have changed. But great detours were necessary to recognize this as the right way. I had to learn to believe in myself and rediscover myself. So, trust your inner voice and listen carefully to the extent to which your project suits you.

The pursuit of one's own goals is comparable in some respects to the construction of a house. There, after a few interviews with the client, a first draft is prepared. All the details, wishes, function programs and possibilities for expansions are already in contain. If you think through all the topics intensively, in the beginning, you save an incredible amount of energy, time and money in the course of the project.

What is the next step? The plan is changed, turned upside down, dismembered and reassembled. After about 3 months and 6 planning meetings, the plan almost looks the way it did at the beginning. The difference, however, is that the client is now certain that he has made the right decisions. He has presented all eventualities from all possible perspectives and has almost come to the same result as in the beginning.

This pre-run can be nerve-racking, but it improves the further project sequence enormously. The client is convinced to get the optimum out of it. During the construction phase, he will hardly ever make any changes. This is so important because changes in the process are much more expensive and time-intensive than in the planning phase.

Regarding your goals, this means taking your time, disassembling your goals, and asking yourself if they really fit you. You can reach any goal, no matter how unrealistic it may be, but do not deceive yourself. Otherwise, after a few years, you will realize the mistake and be frustrated.

Do your goals match your basic conditions?

Create a portfolio of traits that you want to follow on a daily basis. Define the framework in which you feel comfortable. For example, write down the things that you can look forward to every day or that you are proud of.

Can you imagine doing these points on your way to the goal? And above all, after you have achieved your goals?

A few suggestions from my self-check:

> The first hour of the day belongs only to me. I use them for meditation and gymnastics.

> I work with my own schedule, in my own rhythm.

> I wear the clothes I want to wear without constraints.

> I do sports daily.

> I have time for holidays with my children in all school holidays.

> I have free weekends.

> I laugh more than once every day.

> I have successful people full of joy around me, from whom I can learn, and who carry me on my way.

> I learn all the things that interest me from the best teachers.

> I am grateful for what I already have, and I am not jealous of others.

> I live daily in the feeling: there is enough for everyone.

> I would like to say every evening: I have given my best today.

Do your goals and ideas match your daily life?

Ask yourself the right questions!

At this point, questions often are the following:

> Do I have to do all of this in order to achieve my goals?

> How am I supposed to do this?

How does a question like this make you feel? The formulation of the question already builds a certain resistance against the goal or task. We connect the solution immediately with additional work, which is negatively occupied. We would have liked to reach the destination, but the way to get there seems to be exhausting. However, we often have to solve these problems. We are doing this with reluctance, and so the effort is actually higher and the result is most likely worse.

> How can I reach my goals in the shortest period of time with the best possible results?

> In a way that the work I have to do seems easy and fun at the same time?

How does this question feel? Of course, you will now say, "Yes, yes, if it is a meaningful task, it makes me happy. But mostly I get tasks that are useless in my opinion." I can not contradict you. But this is precisely the core subject of this book: How do we get to a point where our tasks and their meaning are defining themselves as often as possible? It is only then that it's easier for us to tackle major tasks and to solve them successfully.

Back to the question: For most people, the second way to phrase these questions sounds much more pleasant, because it does not build up any resistance that we would have to overcome. Instead, it immediately goes into the solution mode. How can I make this the fastest and the best- that already suggests that I can do it in any case. This gives us confidence. The question immediately raises thoughts about a quick, successful and pleasant solution.

These are the best starting conditions for a successful project!

The quality of the questions determines which solutions we find. The questions are the origin of all paths, they determine with how much joy I will solve the respective task.

In this second kind of questioning, we place our subconscious mind in the best possible way. As a faithful worker, it will sift through all the corners of our brain, and it will also consult other sources to find answers to the question. It is now looking for good solutions. And good solutions bring success.

In the first question, "How can I reach my goals?", It searches and finds a thousand things that it believes have to be done. This results in a to-do list that will not end.

KEY 5

GETTING STARTED!

"All beginnings are easy, it is the last steps that are
the most difficult and also those most rarely trodden"
Goethe

If you have made it to this point, you can be proud of yourself. Most people start full of vim and vigor to do something new, but just as quickly they lose interest again. This is due to the fact that they do not know exactly what they want, and can certainly not say why they want it.

The other point is, as funny as it may sound: they do not begin. I know this from myself. In some areas, it is easy for me to start, for example, in craft activities. This is a hobby, I know how to do it, everyone trusts my skills, I have only had good experiences with it, and it is easy to visualize. A project is planned, executed, completed. Goal reached, next one, please!

Let us, therefore, take a few examples in which the beginning is harder for us, and let's consider how we can still make it work.

Eliminate back pain

Back pain now plagues almost everyone. A lot can be done about this.

The first measure is to find out the cause and to consider who can help me.

Physiotherapists are good contacts here. You will create an individual training program, and soon you can begin with small exercises at home.

From my experience, such small, often repeated exercises are much more efficient than big workouts in the gym. They are also cheaper. So if you want to meet friends for a lot of money and want to be seen on imposing devices, go to the gym. If you are looking for something that will help you in the long term, you can incorporate a few inconspicuous exercises into your everyday life.

You can do it at any time without much effort: during the lunch break – sometimes even at the workplace – and certainly in the morning and in the evening at home. Training is body hygiene. For each of us, it is self-evident to wash our faces and brush our teeth in the morning. This should apply to strength and endurance training as well. The time for this must be regarded as an essential part of everyday life.

Go to the physiotherapist of your trust once a month. Take the time to ask your questions. Formulate them as I did under "Ask the right questions".

As described above. Ask for the cause and solution. Do not waste time questioning the symptoms.

If you are pain-free after two months, the further stages of your health will be even more enjoyable. Also, remember to document your exercises and successes in your "Book of Life". These are the steps on the way to success.

Reduce overweight

For many people, the next important stage is the weight reduction.

Again, the key question is, "What can I do now to achieve the desired condition and have fun with it?"

Clarify the reason for your overweight. Almost always this is very simple: you eat or drink too many unhealthy things at the wrong time. You don't believe me and are annoyed by my brazen statement?

Do yourself a favor: Prove the opposite.

Write about what you eat and what you drink over seven days. A small table is very helpful here. Always carry this table with you. Invest in seven pages and do it for one week.

My personal consumption of foods and drinks

Day Time	Drink	Amount	Food	Amount
00:00 a.m.				
01:00 a.m.				
02:00 a.m.				
03:00 a.m.				
04:00 a.m.				
05:00 a.m.				
06:00 a.m.				
07:00 a.m.				
08:00 a.m.				
09:00 a.m.				
10:00 a.m.				
11:00 a.m.				
12:00 a.m.				
01:00 p.m.				
02:00 p.m.				
03:00 p.m.				
04:00 p.m.				
05:00 p.m.				
06:00 p.m.				
07:00 p.m.				
08:00 p.m.				
09:00 p.m.				
10:00 p.m.				
11:00 p.m.				

You can also find this table at the following link:

www.christianschwarz.net/buecher

For further information on nutrition, please refer to the chapter "Secure your energy supply".

Bring this list with you to a nutritionist and get qualified advice. You will be surprised at what he will say after finding his breath again. "Normally you would have to be dead," is often the standard reaction. But most of us still live and are wondering why everything is getting more and more difficult, why it is tweaking here and pulling there.

Love cold calling

Cold calling is also a tricky topic for many. You might ask now, "Why is it so hard for me?" And you will perhaps get the answer from within yourself: "People are so unfriendly, it's embarrassing to me ..." Instead, ask "What can I do to attract new customers in a way that makes me happy?"

In particular, if we are only partially satisfied with the product we have to offer, it is almost impossible to achieve success here. The process is exhausting, gets stuck again and again and costs endless power. If so, consider how you could offer benefits for your customers with this product, and prove it to them during the call or appointment.

If you can not develop a convincing benefit for your potential customer, check the product or the target group. It is very frustrating, despite great exertion and overcoming constant cancellations. It is much more comfortable to bring the right product to the right address at the right time with the right message. With the commitments and the resulting resources, further optimization measures can take place. For example, you can set someone for the cold bill, if you want.

More on the topics product description, target group definition, and promulgation of your

"Embassy", you will find in the chapter "Optimize your products".

These were typical examples that can be applied to your situation. Ask yourself for each of your goals: "What can I do to achieve the desired final state on a path that gives me pleasure?" Through the right questions, you will find your way.

Ask for solutions, not problems!

What resistance do we expect?

Resistance and failure are often indicators that something is not quite right. Often our own goal is not quite clear to us. So ask yourself again and again: What can I improve about my goal and optimize my performance so that I can reach my goal more easily and have fun?

Sometimes, however, envy and disgrace are also the cause. Here too, you can ask yourself the question: "What should I keep in mind so that these people are no longer envious of me?" "How could I improve my behavior towards them?"

Here, however, one has to distinguish whether the envy is selfish or rather results from unintentional admiration. Some people should then not be involved in further thoughts because they will always find something that could harm your success. It is important for you, that you are convinced of your own way and have a clear picture of your goal.

Do not try to convince other people, especially friends and family, of your ideas. Just show them the benefits that this idea, this goal, will have for them too. Also tell them that you love them, and what priorities you put. It could happen that the life partner or the children become jealous of the project and sabotage it consciously or unconsciously.

Further resistances occur in the form of deflections. Self-doubt and fear are very high in the course. You can find more information in the chapter "Distractions".

It is important that you are sure of your cause and start. Your goal is known, whether you then also immediately start in the right direction is secondary. A plane always starts against the wind, no matter where it is to fly. It is only with the movement, when the air moves forward, that the control can work and bring the aircraft to the target course. On the ground, the steering wheel has no effect.

Let's not waste our time with convictions

How much energy I have used to convince friends or strangers of my actions. It was a search for external confirmation and security.

Again and again, we meet dissatisfied people, stiff in their weariness. They will doubt every new idea and make a thousand objections, just as a matter of principle. They take our vigor as an attack on their own sluggish lifestyle. Whether consciously or unconsciously - these people will do everything they can to prevent our success.

But even with friends, we sometimes realize that they are moving in a different direction than we do. Our interests, our conversation topics, are slowly diverging. It would be nonsensical to blame someone. But we should take it into account. Otherwise, it can happen that these friends also sow doubts, especially in moments when we are particularly dependent on encouragement. We need to carefully weigh what we tell about our goals, and when we do it.

If you are on the road, you should document your way. Because sometimes we get the impression that nothing precedes. Then doubts and thoughts of failure arise. Anxiously you ask yourself: What have I done so far? These doubts are also often used against your plans. "I told you it wouldn't work, you didn't believe me ..." - such sentences should be known to everyone.

Then it is good to be able to browse through your own book of life and to read how far you have already come. There we find all the obstacles that we have already overcome, where we have grown, and which have ultimately helped us to come that far. That gives us courage.

How do we convince someone to get up the summit if he likes the valley? We can only talk enthusiastically. Everyone needs to be selfish. Above all, we mustn't let ourselves be kept in the valley. The villagers will be able to name a thousand reasons why it is more beautiful here than on the cold and dangerous mountain.

The path to the goal is paved with dry periods and obstacles.

> *Obstacles and difficulties are the steps we need to climb on our way up.* Nietzsche

Summary

Through your goals, you have determined what you want. You have worked out the reasons why you need to achieve your goals.

You have seen methods that help you start achieving your goals. It is important to start the first activities out of the emotion, to get the wheel rolling. But before speeding up and uncontrollably bouncing against a wall, a few considerations about route planning are useful.

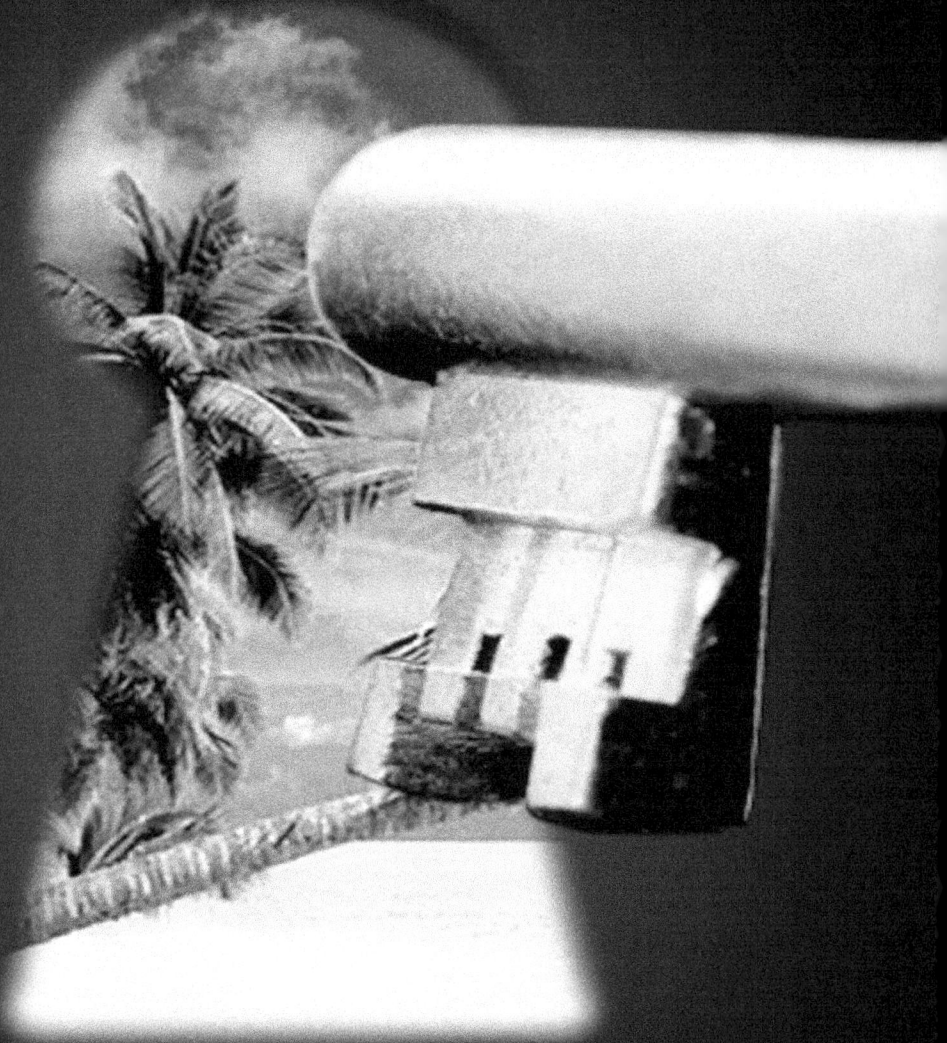

KEY 6

PLANNING

What will I achieve by what time, with what effort,
in what quality?

For the figurative imagination, the construction industry is a grateful area. Imagine you have decided to build a house. You know the room schedule, you know roughly what your house should look like, and you have good reasons why you absolutely need it. You have extensively informed yourself and collected many prospectuses. Do you think it would make sense to buy the first bricks or to order the windows?

It is extremely important to get started immediately and to get some information. But to be successful in the long term, you need good plans that show you in advance what you need to look out for. Although the planning effort may initially be high, you can be sure: through a solid planning process, you can reduce your overall effort drastically and also increase your chances of success in all areas.

Holding and achieving the desired result is only
possible if you have a qualified planning.

Who didn't experience it yet: Full of vigor, we are reaching for new tasks. We start here, go on there. One thing works, the other does not. Then we need information here and some item from the construction store there ... For complex projects, you will quickly get lost with this method. Much time is invested in details that are of little importance to the overall project. Other areas are completely neglected, because we do not really want to do them anyway. Slowly the enthusiasm subsides, the time is short and many tasks are still untouched.

In the course of time, other things become more important, and so we withdraw our attention more and more from our "construction site". The project remains unfinished, and even worse, it has cost energy and time. Even as an unfinished building, it still draws energy from us. Because it makes us feel dissatisfied.

Maybe we can also achieve some good results in this way. Frequently, however, the price is higher than imagined, since the success was costly with much idle time, additional costs and loss of interfaces. Lack of coordination and ambiguous notions of necessary investment often tarnish the supposed success.

In order to ensure that we think of all relevant things, that we have deadlines and always have an overview of the cost situation, planning these things is essential in advance. It does not matter whether it is your goal to build a house or go Christmas shopping, a project-specific planning always saves you time, money and nerves.

Timetable

Let's begin to plan our schedule.

When is my move-in date? When do I want to reach my goal? From this date, you have to count backward. It is possible to give an approximate end date based on experiences and plausibility considerations, even though I don't know yet at how long the individual measures and thus the project will last. The end date can be ambitious, which means that all parties involved are required, but not overwhelmed. It is then used as a point of reference in order to develop further planning and to confirm this end date, which is assumed from experience. If necessary, it can now be corrected.

If we begin differently by first arranging all the necessary measures loosely, then to see which date is finally going to be the end date, this is certainly set later than with the first method.

Obviously, the end date is not postponed when it comes to getting gifts in time for a birthday or Christmas. A good schedule includes fixed points and milestones that must be adhered to. Taking these milestones into account, a schedule is being developed that coordinates the dependencies of individual areas in time.

Changes, additions, and shifts are almost always the cases. To ensure that their effects do not change the entire term situation, so-called free buffer times are installed. This means that if one or the other action moves, this can be buffered in time without the next milestone or even the end date being endangered.

In addition, the schedule takes the necessary resources as well as holiday and seasons into account. Resources are, for example, other companies or persons that we need for the execution and which must also be available for the desired period.

Depending on the project, the scheduling is developed in different degrees of detail. A general overview of the entire project can be found in the rough timetable. This is followed by more and more detailed planning, right up to schedules, which then coordinate the sequence in a very narrow time window during the final phase. These lists always mean stress and it is important to avoid them if possible through good planning in the run-up.

One question I have often heard is, "I have my final date, what do I need a detailed schedule for?" Imagine you have to get Christmas gifts. The end date is clear. But if you can't manage to buy all the gifts in time because of too many distractions in the "calm" pre-Christmas time the, you can get problems. For example, a certain gift is no longer available or it has a longer delivery time. Then gift shopping can be very stressful. Usually, it will also be more expensive if you have no alternatives and no time.

A thought-out schedule takes account of the longer delivery times in the Christmas shop and keeps you at risk. Better, it tells you in time when you should start. One look is enough and you know you have to start Christmas shopping this week. There is still time to look for an alternative gift. An exchange or longer delivery times cause no stress. The whole project "Christmas shopping" is completely relaxed, stress-free and perhaps even cheaper. If you only want to set a date for purchasing, you do not need a particularly sophisticated schedule yet. But as soon as it comes to getting the Christmas tree, wrapping the gifts, baking cookies, inviting guests, to buy wine and drinks and integrating it into the normal daily routine, a schedule appears to be more sensible.

A good schedule gives you an overview of what needs to be done when. This also makes it easier for you to see what things you might be able to do because you have to go to the city anyway.

Forward-looking scheduling reduces costs and stress
and improves quality

In the case of more complex things such as the construction of a house, the plans of all parties involved are synchronized on schedule. A so-called planning schedule ensures that the specialist planners work out the respective plans and make them available on time.

An implementation schedule then coordinates the craftsmen and suppliers.

If for example, you are redecorating a school, you have to do noisy work on the lesson-free time (yes, I know if you are a parent, you know that this is not the case at your children's school …).

If you do not match all these things exactly, it will be difficult to the end date. Also because you have no way to measure how far you are already. Are we on schedule or not? If you can not measure something, you will not be able to control it either. If we do not know where in the ocean we are sailing, we can hardly set the course for the goal.

Calendars in Outlook etc. are very good for the day-to-day business. However, they are not suitable for a project plan. Because they are not intended to represent connections, surveys, and dependencies.

A simple and very clear representation is the bar chart. Here the activities are described in the left column and the periods for the execution of the activities are indicated on the right according to the selected time scale. Connections and dependencies can be set. Thus, for example, one immediately recognizes the effect of a deadline shift at the beginning of the project on interim deadlines or even on the final deadline. This is especially necessary for complex projects with many dependencies, which is essential and enormously time-saving. Microsoft Project is one of many programs that provide great services.

A tip on the edge: The immediate recognition of possible consequences with time shifts can be used very well for argumentation in order to not have to tolerate a delaying measure. Some project participants are very creative, in order to gain as much time as possible for themselves. They are constantly trying to shift their contribution to the project further back on the schedule. If you let that happen as project manager, because you are a nice person and want to help the others, that can result in a lot of extra work for you. Here, too, the practice has shown that an enormous amount of energy and time can be saved if, disjoined by emotional discussions, you can refer to the tight schedule and make the consequences of a delay visible immediately.

Last but not least: do not forget the breaks! In the chapter "Secure your energy supply", we will discuss the importance of breaks, rest and regeneration times. Just before you do so: You have to integrate breaks as an integral part of your schedule and comply with them. This greatly increases your chances of staying on the schedule. Do not cheat yourself: Break times are not free buffer times.

Budget plan

Each goal needs some form of investment. Usually, this is time and money. The budget for time is defined in the schedule. There is the budget plan for the finances. Whether you are building a house, building a new production line in your manufacture, training as a flight captain, or bringing the children to music lessons at different times – all this means investing money and time.

A cost calculation is useful for every major goal.

For example, if you have a journey as a goal, you will know very early what it is going to cost. The flights and the hotel are clear, a few percent additional costs and purchases to it ... and you already have an amount, which is to be expected.

If the goal is to build a house, the investment is very interesting. Because the amounts are usually much higher than on a trip. And there are many,

many individual components that need to be calculated. A layman can't do specific work, he is dependent on professional help. For this reason, a small additional investment in an "expert in costs" is very advisable (architects are often not; because their profession is the design, the creativity – and that often conflicts with the costs).

Your plan is only as good as the data with which you fed it. It is therefore advisable to plan with a certain percentage of unforeseen additional investments.

If you want to build a house for 500,000 euros, and there will be a 10% extra charge on the end of the construction period due to the additions you have not calculated,

50.000 Euro represents a great challenge. There are stress and delays in the construction process, resulting in further costs and time loss.

I don't want to scare you, but if goals are to lead to changes in life, this often entails a great effort, both financially and temporally. To consider these investments in a realistic way, to get advice from outside and to carry out their own plausibility checks, again and again, is a good way to get an overview and keep it during the projects.

Quality planning

What quality do I want to achieve? If you have ever attended seminars on personality development, you know that there is often the talk of the "best", the "finest". This is basically right. Only often it is not clear to visualize. That is why we are at first very hard to believe in it. Here, too, we need a clear objective in individual areas that can be reconciled with the overall system. What do we want to be of best quality, why would we like it? Which areas are sufficient for the time being in normal quality but can be improved or supplemented later?

You plan your dream home and have a very exact idea of your bathroom. From the tiles, the faucets, the bathtub, and the surround music system. At the same time, you want to have real wood parquet throughout the house.

Normally, only a cost estimation by the architect is present during this phase, which however may have a high tolerance and therefore is not a reliable basis for calculation. Therefore, I recommend you to invest a relatively small amount before the beginning of the project or before starting the project, and to have the costs calculated as precisely as possible.

If you follow this advice, you know from the budget plan and the cost calculation that parquet and dream bath is not possible at the same time. While this is not optimal, you can now make clear decisions and be sure that you have taken all the options. It is only when you have an overview of all trades and their costs that such fact-based decisions are possible. They bring safety and relaxation to the entire project.

In this case, it is clear: the bathroom is built as you imagine it. Tiles, shower, and bathtub are later only with very high expenditure and much dirt again to exchange. The real wood parquet has to wait. In the case of floor coverings, retrofitting or even replacing is possible after a few years at a reasonable cost. From my own experience, I can say that we would have been better off waiting with the parquet a few years and first lay down a more favorable carpet. Then the parquet would have spared a lot of dents and scratches due to dropped toys ...

Resource planning

What resources do we have available for our development, our plans? Resources include, of course, money, time, knowledge, but also contacts, ideas, experiences, friends and not least the family.

Because you can start whatever you want – if your partnership and the education of the children are important to you, then you have to include those aspects into your plans as well. When these relationships break away, you lose a lot of energy, time and money.

Very often you are not aware of your resources. It is similar to the beautiful and precious experiences, which are getting lost somewhere in the compressed retrospect.

Without appropriate planning, it is hardly possible to calculate the necessary investments, the time required and the available resources. The following questions are very helpful when it comes to discovering, evaluating, and scheduling available resources:

> Are my knowledge and skills enough for the project?

> What else should I learn because it is very important for my project?

> Who do I need to support?

> Who can I ask if it becomes difficult?

> How much time can I invest? Per day, per week?

> How much money can I make available for the project?

> How strongly can I burden my environment without causing problems?

> *The framework for a successful project is the interplay of the four major areas of time planning, budget planning, quality planning and resource planning.*

Minimising risk

Just as qualified planning increases the likelihood of achieving its goals, the risk of making losses decreases equally. There is no project without risk. But you can shape the framework in such a way that this risk is minimized. Just think about the morning bath ritual. Even with the wet razor, you could really seriously cut yourself, would there not be the protection wires to minimize the risk. You could also stumble over the cat in the dark and break your nose on the sink. The electric light and the light switches that are planned in the right place considerably reduce this danger.

There are always factors that may have been inadequately considered or circumstances that you have no influence on. However, they can be defused by first-class planning. In the schedule, there are the free buffer times, in the budget plan the dormant reserves and in the resource planning perhaps the good friend, which jumps to your help if necessary.

It only becomes critical when several factors remain unobserved, which then turn into problems in the execution phase. If time, money and other resources are running out at the same time, the project can become very expensive and in the worst case even fail.

Reaching a goal is always a project.

Summary

Project preparation and planning is always very time-consuming. However, this is far less than the effort required for corrections and damage mitigation in projects that were not well thought through.

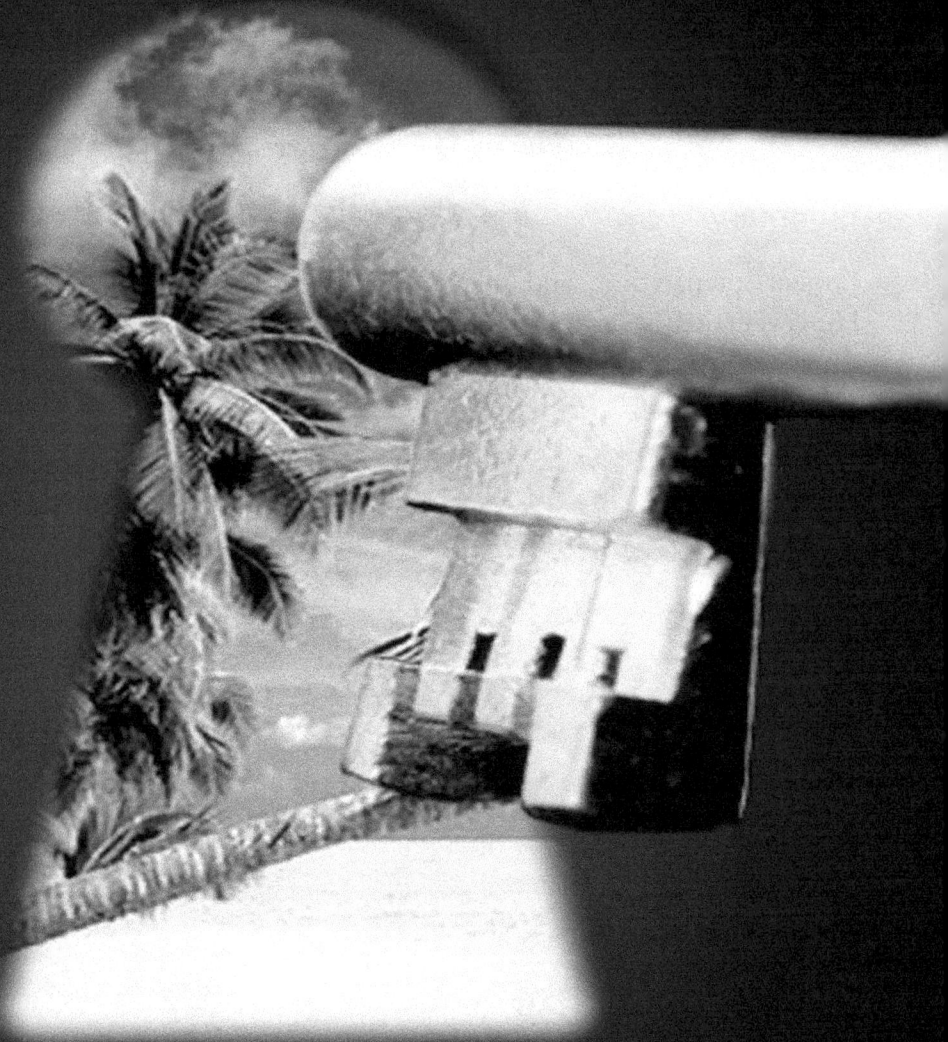

KEY 7

STOP THE WASTE OF TIME, MONEY AND MOTIVATION

Let's take a look into the working life. All of the examples are approximately the same as described here. They can serve as thought-provoking ideas and show us what may be the reason for the fact that the tasks pile up more and more and the success experiences become less and less. Why we sometimes we like we were stuck in a hamster wheel and our motivation decreases. Be assured, these are not individual cases.

Failure to identify the basis

Production-supporting software should be provided for a new production facility. After receipt of the order and confirmation, it turned out that the basic determination was not sufficient. During the order processing, it was obvious that the delivered software could not communicate with the existing machines by default. This had not been verified during the basic determination.

The result was a delay of about 5 months as well as an additional development effort for 3 persons of a total of approx. 5 weeks. In addition, the development manager was bound to the project for at least 15 hours. And it had to be purchased test software for 6,000 euro, in order to be able to check all functionalities before the second delivery. This software was not planned for the order and therefore not calculated.

In addition, important developments in other areas remained on the line due to the additional work. This, in turn, resulted in delays, work obstructions and additional costs for employees and other customers, which must be assumed again at least on this scale.

The resulting additional costs exceed the calculated profit. In addition, customer satisfaction has decreased. Not only with this one customer, but also with those customers who were also affected by the bottlenecks. The resulting costs sum up to a total of 40,000 – 50,000 euros. Here the damage caused by the loss of follow-up orders is just as little considered as the time loss of one's own employees due to permanent delays and additional meetings. The costs incurred by the customer as a result of a loss of production have also not yet been taken into account.

Disregard of the customers' interests

A completely wrong calculated project blocks all other projects. The reason for this is an unclear coordination between the customer and the contractor, as well as a lack of recording and documentation of the customer's request. In addition, there are unforeseen development issues for product properties that have been contractually agreed on. Due to the lack of communication and opacity of the product structures, sales have assumed that these functionalities are available. Since this was not the case, they must now be developed at the contractor's expense.

In addition, two persons are additionally busy with error analysis and damage elimination over a period of 5 months, 2 days per week on site. An additional, unpaid work of about 2 days x 8 hours x 5 months = 80 days.

Due to the size of the contract and the related contractual penalty, this project has top priority. Therefore, many appointments for other projects have to be canceled at short notice, which leads to further customer dissatisfaction. For the employees in the field service, it means even more frequent changes of location, which leads to disproportionate travel times and therefore unproductive time. This time is missing for the preparation of customer appointments. Therefore, on-site work can often not be completed. The disposition is constantly busy with balancing the schedule and the customer satisfaction. Project schedules from other projects are postponed without the consequences being assessed. In effect, it is a vicious circle of shifts that frustrates all employees and customers. The daily pace is not reached and this leads to great dissatisfaction and stress at all levels.

It is easy to see how important it is to carry out a qualified basic analysis. Here, one must think very conscientiously about all eventualities and finally discuss them with the client. It has to be documented in detail, what OBJECTIVES he actually pursues with the investment. Only when we know its WHY, we are able to find the right products for its solution.

Meetings lasting for hours

Internal meeting, Tuesday 9:00 am 7 participants, duration 2 hours. Agenda is missing, no time to create a meeting log. Yes, there is such a thing.

The review of an order confirmation is displayed. The person in contact with the customer is not present. The result is long speculation about the main formulations in the quotation. While six people are waiting for the missing information by telephone inquiry, six people are waiting in the meeting room. The co-worker is not available, so you finally start to discuss the next case. In the middle of the discussion of this point, the recall of the co-worker comes in. Again the work of seven people is interrupted. And the caller had to leave other tasks. After lengthy debate, unfortunately, he can not give any final answers to all questions. He promises, however, to clarify this immediately with the customer. The second callback occurs after the end of the meeting and interrupts the current work of the department head.

The result of the discussion is a postponement of the decisions on essential points. Directly about 7 hours of working time are lost and there are still countless more. Because no information can be given, no clear decisions can be made. The already scheduled deadlines must, therefore, be postponed.

Regular discussions will turn into endless discussions because decisive persons are not involved in time and because no one in the meeting knows exactly which information has to be collected from the customer

Unclear work instructions

In technical field service and also in the craft sector, the tasks must be exactly defined. It is just as important to know the basic conditions on the spot before the deadline. This sounds absolutely logical and should be self-evident – only in reality does it often look different.

The next time you pass a construction site, you will see that at least one of them is on the phone. Usually, one or two colleagues are standing by and waiting for the outcome of the conversation (I always wonder what they did before the mobile phone was invented).

In particular, executives and supervisors are asked to ensure the most comprehensive possible preparation. This must be discussed with the executing staff and the concrete objectives of local meetings or measures must be presented clearly and in writing. In addition, the time for preparation for the staff must be planned and the quality of this preparation must be checked at least initially. Because everyone knows something different. And negligence on this point is one of the main reasons for failed projects or inefficient appointments.

In addition, the measures must be discussed in advance with the customer. When it comes to more complex topics, this is usually done in the presence of the performer.

If several people are traveling together to an appointment, the documentation of the day's destinations is certainly not a waste of time. If one renounces this, often the following happens: One relies on another: "He will already know what to do". In order to not seem clueless, he also pretends he knows it. The result is clear. No sooner arrival at the customer's location, you call the control center to get the missing information. Who is then interrupted in his work, you can imagine...

The loss of time on the ground due to a lack of preparation or a bad basic determination is very expensive for several reasons:

> Own time was inefficient.

> The same applies to the time of the customer who also had to leave the appointment.

> Other technicians and the project managers are torn out of their work and must be available at short notice for queries.

> Finally, the customer begins to doubt the employee's professional knowledge. This loss of confidence can lead to a loss of the customer in the medium term and in case of repeated errors.

I can understand, if you now object: "This doesn't work in practice, I can not hold meetings all the time." But you can do this if the discussions briefly and objectively represent the framework and objectives. And if they are documented in writing. This documentation is handed over to the executors in the form of a protocol. Often a few points are enough.

This procedure means much less effort. And it is much more cost-effective than to carry out improvements, organize shifts and fight against contract penalties.

The modern communication possibilities can support us here wonderfully. Keep short video conferences, not too expensive, show a few photos of the location, or talk to your employees and the client at the same time. Communicate with each other, so that before the appointment everyone is on the same level of information. Record the call and send it as a log before the appointment. These days, this is very easy with smartphones etc. invest here. Your employees will be happy to get "cool" devices paid by the boss, and you will have a significantly reduced time requirement.

The most important thing, however, is that all parties agree on the results to be achieved and the time frame for this and that they have confirmed this in writing. For larger projects, this is usually the standard. But the smaller ones are treated very negatively.

Check your cost-benefit factor with regard to the order sum and the planned order period. I would not be surprised if you invest the famous 80% of your time in small orders that represent a maximum of 20% of your profit.

„Do you have a minute?"

There are not just a few department managers who are confronted with this question throughout the day, consuming more than 80% of their regular working hours. The actual work is then done in the overtime hours.

By topics that arise "short-term" and "must be treated" immediately ", a great time loss arises. The subject matter is usually known for a long time, but no one has ever really accepted it. The spontaneous discussion, mostly due to "fire alarms" from the customer, does not bring a lasting result, but only short-term "cooling". Unequaled, unplanned procedures in the short-term processing result in additional quality and time losses.

Furthermore, appointments for third parties are also postponed, which triggers a chain reaction. Again, we fail to provide a clear definition of when and in what form requests can be made.

> *In principle, "interrupters" and thus "time-thieves"*
> *should be stopped before they can ask the question*
> *"Do I disturb?"*

We should make these "interrupters" appear only at fixed times. In addition, they need to bring their concerns, in writing, in a nutshell, and with a suggested solution with them.

The following information should be included in the written preparation:

> What is it about?

> What can be improved in the current situation?

> Which solution do I have?

> How do we benefit from this solution and what benefits does the customer have?

> When will the problem be solved?

In many cases, the conference is no longer necessary after such considerations. Or it can be reduced to a few details and thus to a minimum.

Otherwise, it has proved useful to have fixed times for general questions twice a week. After application, they can be processed quickly.

Each employee should have an overall agenda for themselves so that he does not forget the questions that arise during the day until the deadline. So he does not have to go to the department manager for every question.

Summary

Project preparation and project planning need time. The amortization period, however, is very short and the profit increases enormously.

KEY 8

TECHNICAL TIME MANAGEMENT

To-do lists

For 4,000 years we have been using the same system to accomplish our tasks. In the meantime, however, the world's knowledge doubles every 5 to 10 years. By some new possibilities, we were completely taken over, for example, by constant availability via the Internet and the associated technologies. Practically overnight, an expectation has arisen with regard to our reaction speed, which we can not match with our learned behavioral patterns. For our way of structuring and processing the tasks is the same as it was 4,000 years ago. Even though we usually keep them in to-do lists these days.

It is completely indifferent whether you create these lists by PC, smartphone or on paper. The lists are always longer because as soon as you have finished a point, two new ones are added.

The name of the list already reveals what is to be expected: a lot of work. But we do not want work, we want results. Therefore our list should be called "list of results". If we focus on the tasks, we get more and more of them.

> *Successful people do not ask themselves: "What do I have to do".*

Instead, you ask yourself the following questions:

> What do I want to achieve?

> Why do I want to achieve it?

> What steps are necessary?

With this question, we do not focus on what we have to do but on our goal. We do not focus on the "to-do", but on the desired result. Wherever we draw our attention, we are also guided by our thoughts, words, and works. The subconscious contributes to this and also looks forward to the results that promise joy and happiness. It helps us to discover new ways to the goal that the brain has not yet thought of. It has the clear command from the brain to achieve this result. Thus, all our systems are working towards the result. If on the other hand, we concentrate our attention, our actions and the instructions to our subconsciousness on to-do lists, one point after another is done, but many possibilities and alternatives remain undetected. This is due to the fact that from this perspective it is not possible to see where the trip should go. The overall plan is not covered by the subconscious, and so it can not help us to find solutions, but only stupid point by point.

Just think of the shopping list that your wife wrote for you. You have done everything, but the question of whether or not you have also brought some cream, answer with a clear no. Cream was not on the list. If you knew that the list was intended for eating with friends, with a dessert of plum cake, you would probably have come along with the idea of bringing cream.

In principle, a to-do list works like a conversation in which one only responds exactly to what the other asks, and does not consider what he is going to do. "Can you tell me how late it is?" - "Yes." The answer is correct, but it does not help you. You have even more "work" with the next question, and so you consume time and energy, and the tasks become more and more.

If you talk without any connection about the things that are on your list, you will not be able to get any great help from outside. If, on the other hand, you declare that you are planning a trip to Hawaii and, therefore, have to deal with all these points, it may happen that your opposite says: "I was just there. Should I give you some tips? ". The quality of the information is most likely much better than what you would have achieved by processing your to-do list. You also saved a lot of time.

If you have internalized this, you have a to-do list as a thought-support. It helps you keep in mind, what results you would like to achieve today. However, make sure to add to each point very briefly, WHY you want to reach it. You are on the winning track.

Clean your desk

Exclusively having the documents on the desk that you are working on at the moment is one of the first tips in many courses on office organization. Only then can the whole concentration be focused on the current topic. Now you might say, "I don't mind. I can work as well on an overloaded desk."Congratulations, if so. However, numerous scientific investigations show that virtually every human being is distracted from things in his environment. In particular, unfinished things, the sight of which can provoke incriminating thoughts. Of a piece of decoration, which is always on the table, we are certainly less distracted than from a mountain of files, loose paper, or books.

It is easy to explain why it takes more energy to focus on something when there are distractions for the eyes or the ears. Imagine the following scene: you look out into the sea, the waves glide calmly and regularly to the beach. You are watching a seagull pulling its tracks. You pay attention to its wing stroke and long sail phases. On the descent, the ascent, and the change of direction. You observe it until it has disappeared on the horizon. Do you think you've been watching a seagull in Hamburg?

Surely you will do your work well. But it is the little things that make it difficult to keep the focus, always branching off energy somewhere and interrupting the concentration. Just think of the dripping water tap, how much water disappears in the course of a day. Likewise, all of the tiny distractions evade you without realizing it.

Therefore, pay attention to the small things while you
pursue your great goals

Dealing with emails, WhatsApp messages etc.

This is like a drug that spreads rapidly, is initially fun and does not initially cause any visible damage. In certain circumstances, and especially when properly dosed, it can be of great use. But who informs us about risks and side effects? You could only consult your time management or target-finding officer if you have one.

Initially, I have an average of 30 times a day checked my inbox or Outlook has pointed out to me in the inbox. That is, I let myself be disturbed 30 times in my concentration and interrupt the current work. Use only 5 minutes to read and for short answers, are 2.5 hours away. Considering the time we need to get back into our work, we need these five minutes with certainty.

Check yourself to make yourself aware of how often you get torn out of your work. For 2 days, run a list of all the ticks: any interruption is a note on your page. Whether the interruption is wanted or unwanted is not important.

You know all these interruptions, which seem to be always important and urgent and which you must not postpone. The time is fast-paced and usually, a response is expected immediately. For example, three, four, or more emails are going back and forth until a little bit is clarified. Each gets a tick, whether read or written itself. After you've counted the strokes just before the end of the day, consider whether you remember the first 10 news of the day. Think about how many would actually have led to a disaster if they had been unanswered for more than three hours.

My experience has shown that it is less than 10%. With the remaining well 90%, I could easily have saved a few hours of time. Many of them wouldn't have required a reaction at all. And even the important 10% do not usually stop the world from turning.

If our business partners and clients are accustomed to receiving emails or other messages from us at 1:00 pm and 4:00 pm, they are prepared to do so. You can set a time for responses in your communication programs (as a version of the absence note). For really urgent matters, you can specify other ways to reach an emergency. But make clear: only in an emergency!

An example of this is well-organized physiotherapists or doctors. They can not interrupt their work on the patient all the time. Even with a priest, it would be rather unusual if during the mass his mobile phone rings. Although in his case it may well be that life and death are concerned. And do you think a football star will check his messages during a game or during training?

Technically this can be prevented by setting the collection times of messages.

If this is not the case, deactivate at least the acoustic signal and also the visual display for the arrival of messages. For the disturbance begins at the remark. It is like the always too late question: "May I disturb you for a short time?"

If you are less likely to be interrupted, you will soon get better results. You will be able to do much more in higher quality. What is important, however, is that you get the impression that you have achieved something important today. You can safely switch off and enjoy the evening relaxed.

Dealing with social media

Private things do not belong on the internet.

If I can only believe half of what is reported about the systematic scanning and analysis of data, I am no longer surprised that I do not get any offers for eyeglasses. On my Facebook picture, I wear none. What role does this play? The pictures are supposedly searched for eyeglasses and corresponding offers then end up on our screen. What there is from this Bruce Springsteen, I've learned more since I registered it in my Facebook account under music taste. Now, this is relatively harmless information. But some users, especially children, and adolescents, publish much more sensitive data. And unfortunately also appropriate or better inappropriate photos to it. Eventually, the time (if it is not already there) will come, in which our "perfect Internet past" is respected. Salary and reputation are dependent on it, then. Dependencies are created up to the point of blackmail.

I see it equal to tattoos. They are cool, of course, and some of them look quite good. But at some point, many people are no longer so "happy" about the images of their stormy youth. And also the tattoos lose their sharpness on wrinkled skin. Often the motives could not keep pace with the personal development and after a few years, they are seen as embarrassing.

Similar to data on the Internet, you can almost get tattoos away. However, at least one still has the possibility to protect themselves by appropriate clothing before glances. Different on the Internet. Apart from a global "reset" of the data storage – by several hundred atomic bomb flashes or a meteorite impact – the once adjusted data will probably no longer be deleted from the WWW and its backups.

In terms of time competency, social media have similar rules as for email (see "Dealing with emails"). Those who value their time should think carefully about how much they invest in posting and tweeting. Time is our most valuable resource. We can not multiply it, we can only use it better.

For business purposes, things look a little different. Here we can put ourselves on the side of the hunters and test all marketing strategies and surely also generate good business from it. The imagination knows no limits. Nevertheless, it should also be noted here that we should only spread what is honest and substantial.

> *Time is our most precious resource, we can not*
> *multiply it, we can only use it better.*

Conference management

Discussions are a very expensive, but also indispensable means of carrying out projects of all kinds with several participants. Therefore, it is necessary to prepare each meeting well and to go through it quickly. Ultimately, clear results, agreements, deadlines, and responsibilities have to be precisely documented. This sounds logical, but it is not implemented in very few cases.

Control can only be achieved if the meeting manager knows exactly what is to be achieved with this meeting. He must know who he needs, and what documents are necessary. He must know its objectives and these objectives must be consistent with the project plans. Only if he knows what each participant has to do, until when and how much dependencies it is connected, he can lead a qualified meeting.

The meeting manager must provide the meeting points in advance and write them in such a way that each participant knows which documents he or she should bring and how he must prepare himself. If the objectives of each point are clearly presented, the classic excuse "I didn't know that" is in an almost magical way avoided. From a certain level of training and responsibility, everyone can be expected to think about how to implement their points. Of course, he has to know the goals of these points and he has to be able to put his own points on the agenda beforehand. If one of the participants is not prepared or disturbs the meeting through his behavior, then make him leave. If it's your boss, then give him this book.

A further effect, especially in well-trained teams, is that the invited students are already thinking about possible solutions when studying the agenda and they coordinate these in individual discussions with other participants. This includes the timely request for missing documents. This is the ideal case. It occurs more and more frequently when all parties know that they are thereby quickly dismissed from the conference. In addition, they recognize in a well-organized meeting that everything that is asked of them is actually in demand and that it is built on it.

A lot of time is also saved by keeping the initial time exactly and giving everyone who is not punctual the impression that he is disturbing everyone else and is responsible when the end of the discussion shifts backward. The end must be defined as well as the beginning. It is hard to believe what power it takes to keep discussions effective and to get to the point when the end of the meeting is reached. With your agenda, you have a good measuring instrument for how quickly you have to plan. If you are still at point 4 of 15 after half the time, it could be close.

Decisive is the ability of the meeting leader to complete the points, to document them, and then to summarize the decision to reassess the responsibilities and the fixed appointments. This saves all participants the endless phone calls and emails after data despatch. The summary at the end of each point has the advantage that the memory is still fresh. If all points are summarized at the end, this often leads to time-intensive discussions.

The protocol should be sent soon, ideally on the same day. This helps you and also the participants because they are still very familiar with the events. Three days later, far too many things have happened which may be more important or at least seem more important. So you create the "old" protocol "last minute" which makes important things urgently again.

Summary

You can see how much it can cost us when schedules and projects are not adequately prepared. Often the cause is the supposedly missing time. Even a rough post-calculation shows, however, that the bottom line is much higher costs and that more time is consumed than if one takes a long time in advance.

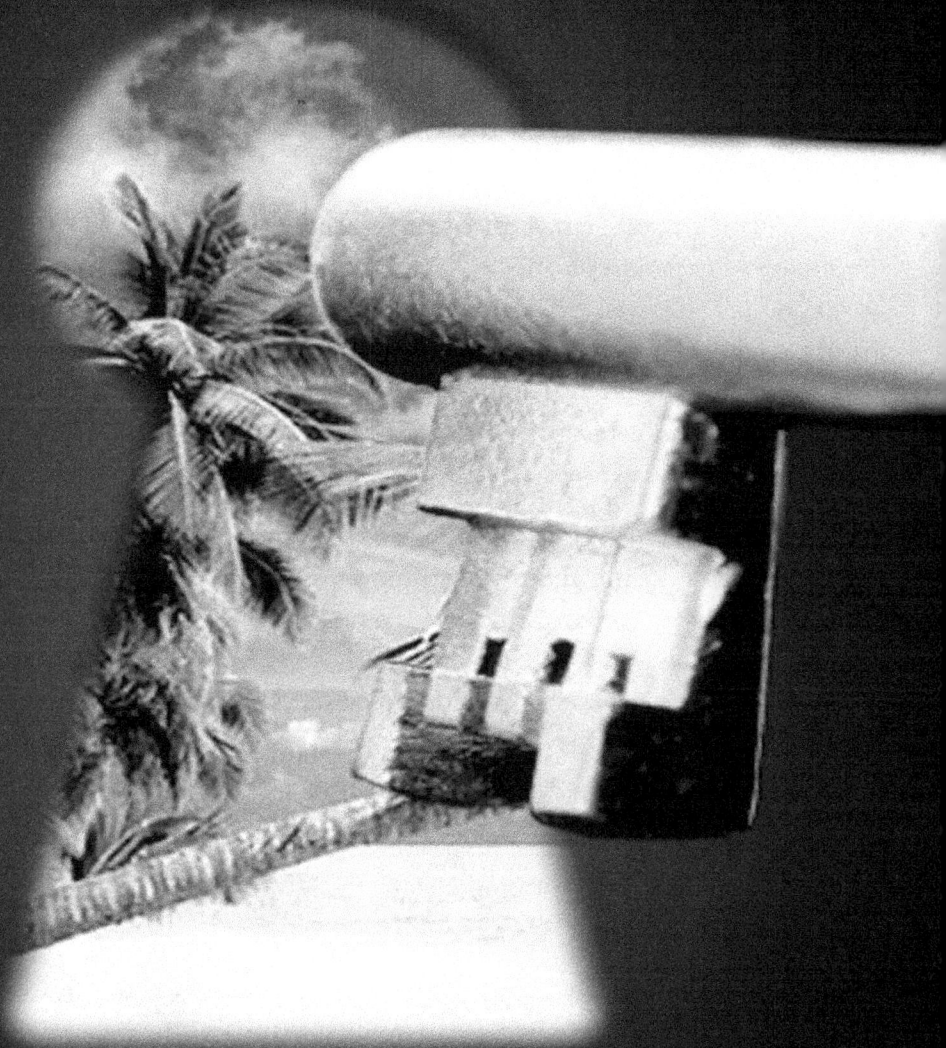

KEY 9

IMPORTANT IS RELATIVE

Again and again, the words "important" and "urgent" emerge. Let us look at what these words have to do regarding our time quota and our stress level.

The flood of information is constantly increasing. And in the form of your smartphone, this information also keeps track of you everywhere. Yes, they shine, hum, ring and vibrate regularly and more frequently into your everyday life. They are also poison for the times when you do not really want to think about any information at all. However, constant availability is expected today. Who has the courage to get out?

Any unplanned interruption will damage your productivity. As a result of the increased time required, you are less and less likely to be able to do your tasks in the working time. The result is clear: the overtime is rising. This is also modern. Anyone who does not work overtime is not considered important, committed and casual. But that is exactly what we want to be! At least we men tend to.

Just think back, what casual Cowboys with Marlboro cigarettes have ridden through the endless expanse. Everyone wanted to be like this. Since, however, the fewest could go to the Wild West, at least they started smoking cigarettes.

The Cowboys of today are the after-work types. Casually dressed, they come to the party after many overtime hours, slightly stressed, but still cheerful.

Since this situation – just like the ride to the Wild West – is again the least contented, the majority of the "everybody" is content with the overtime and the stress and feels relaxed.

We are so programmed that we are even proud to be working overtime and to be stressed. The fact that this results in a psychological burden that can lead to lasting damage is just as much a thing as the health damage caused by smoking. Perhaps in the future, a label will stick to the company door:

Caution - work can be fatal.

Due to the extreme flood of information and the communication pressure, we can not sufficiently reduce the stress with conventional approaches. We have only one option: to decide whether we want to be important or to be successful.

It is our decision! Of course, it entails consequences: It requires a system change! And it does not start with the fact that we are only able to control our SMS three times a day. We will not last long. It is necessary to change our framework conditions! "General conditions" are meant as settings and attitudes in this case.

We need to rethink and clarify ourselves: "I am not a fair game, people can't come with their information and inquiries at any time. I myself determine when I allow information and communication and when I answer whom."

Our stress level is not solely dependent on the amount of work. The point of view from which we look at the particular thing is decisive, the meaning which we give it, and the value which we attach to it.

The extent to which we are satisfied and relaxed with ourselves is essentially dependent on how we assess our daily tasks, how we deal with them and how much time we spend on them.

Many people have thought about this. What Eisenhower has found can also be applied to our time with slight adjustments.

Activities according to importance and urgency

If we assess our activities according to importance and urgency, then the following areas arise:

I   Not important and not urgent → frustration

II   Not important but urgent → stress

III Important and urgent → stress

IV Important but not urgent → relaxation, joy, success

Depending on how long we are in the respective areas, our mood changes.

I   Not important and not urgent → frustration

Reading and writing unimportant SMS, watching TV, surfing the web, playing computer games, reading comments from other people on specific events. Follow the latest news daily and discuss it.

Most people spend much of their lives with things that are neither important nor urgent. Common claim, right? This is also perfectly fine and very social. Hundreds of thousands of jobs are thus secured. However, if you are serious about your time and your achievement, you should be honest with yourself and ask yourself whether this type of employment is actually useful. There is no question that these things belong together, everyone does that. But what priority they have in our lives determines how successful and satisfied we are. None of the above-mentioned things is of direct benefit to us.

In this area is a huge potential of time to find if you want to find it.

II   Not important, but urgent → stress

The area "Not important, but urgent" mainly exists because we see too many things as urgent, or they are made urgent. Many of them are not really urgent.

The question is: how can the number of supposedly urgent tasks be reduced? How urgent is it to actually stare at the moment of the auction end on the Ebay side?

Decide whether your time is more important than the 20 Euro extra charge. The more important you are the object of the auction, the more you can offer. You save a lot of time if you decide in advance for a reasonable price and then let the matter run its course. Those who really care about your time know the decision. They know how to do things that will bring them more than the uncertain "bargain price".

If you manage to reduce the urgency to be online at this moment, you have reduced your stress level and gained more time for other topics.

The consideration of urgency and a clear decision are crucial to whether or not we get stressed.

III Important and urgent → stress

Make business decisions, prepare tax audit, learn for a test,

Preparation of meetings – these issues are important. The moment we learn that we have to be active in some form, these things are usually not urgent. They will do so only when we postpone them. Then we get really stressed. Experience shows that this is true of over ninety percent of things that are important and urgent, causing massive stress. How the timely "start-up" succeeds, you can read in the chapter "Scheduling".

The situation is different in the case of unforeseeable events. An accident – a major actress falls short and has to be replaced. In the Rolling Stones, there would be no Mick Jagger. In such a moment really stress comes up. I would call that fate. It should not be. There is no backup for such a case.

If, on the other hand, a lightning strikes the power line and the process has to be interrupted for a longer period of time, this is again the subject of planning. An emergency power station would have had to be prepared if the event was so extremely important. If it is not, it can also be canceled. Of course this sounds like good-natured. Nevertheless, what could really happen in good planning so that we are massively stressed? How likely is this case?

In business day, important and urgent decisions are constantly being made. Many managers live there, and it will surely not be possible to avoid them. However, you should use one or the other of the previous pages and observe the situation accordingly. You will find that many cases can actually be defused. However, the prerequisite is that we really want it and we do not necessarily want to ride through our lives as a modern "Marlboro Cowboy".

IV   Important but not urgent → relaxation, joy, success

Prepare decisions and meetings in peace, exercise regularly, attend further training courses, schedule projects on time and carry out systematic control routines. Spend time with your family and friends and have a relaxing time. Help your children with their homework. Schedule appointments timely and well prepared...

We feel really comfortable when these important things go hand–in–hand with us. If they do not put pressure on us because we start them in time before they become urgent. This could also be the reason why many things work by themselves in this state.

Meetings are important. Imagine you are preparing the next meeting in peace, clarifying the agenda, and knowing your goals for the individual points you want to reach in the meeting.

Sport and physical fitness are vital. Also, they are not urgent in normal cases. They will not be until the doctor gives you a hint with the "fence post" to keep you from a heart attack. If, from the outset, regular, physical activity is a high priority and a permanent place in your day-to-day work, this topic will not be urgent.

Further education is also not urgent if we carry it out on a regular basis and plan the next appointments in time. Control of the tasks of our employees, customer satisfaction, improvement processes and business results ... everything becomes urgent only if we let things grind and are suddenly forced to act in the short term.

We gain strength from the fourth area, although we are constantly making important decisions and certainly making more and moving than in all other areas. You will be able to play with things that you are proud of and which will bring great benefits to you and others. Through this efficient way of working and living, there is also sufficient inner peace and contentment in order to relax and enjoy the breaks.

However, there is still another danger. Our company is oriented towards permanent employment, or rather, conditioned on it. Someone who is not in stress, is already suspected to do nothing. This is a danger, not to be underestimated, for one's own sense of value, especially when something does not succeed immediately, despite all the ease. In this case, we are very quick to ask ourselves, "What am I doing, am I really enough?" We begin to doubt ourselves and our performance. Stay faithful, browse through your "Book of Life" and read how you've come to a relaxed position. If you can make it visible again and again, then you are protected against this danger and can continue to be on the road to success. If not, you will learn about methods that will get you back on track.

What do we spend our time on?

How stressed we are depends on how much time we spend in each area.

Write down what you do every day, and assign them to one of categories I to IV. Estimate how much time you spend per day or per week in which area.

Consider: Thoughts also cost time. With which thoughts, which in principle bring nothing, do you deal with each day? Here are also thoughts of things that you can not change, such as the weather, football results, scandals of celebrities or problems that are a thing of the past.

> What to do and what do you think about the day?

> How much time do you spend on these activities per day?

> Assign the individual activities to areas I to IV.

Focus on gold nuggets

You ideally spend most of your life with IV activities. These are the gold nuggets. Feel in yourself: how much time would you like to spend in the area IV? I can only speak for myself, but if I manage to experience 60 to 70 percent of my time like that, I'm really in a good mood. My goal is about 80 percent. However, I must admit: this requires a great discipline, and sometimes I simply do not want discipline. But my goals and my reasons for this draw me almost automatically in the right track. It is not urgent now, but it is important to continue to work on it. I know my goals and I like to get a little closer to them every day.

How much **percent** of your time do you spend in the categories I-IV?

Sketch your own circle to make your time division visible.

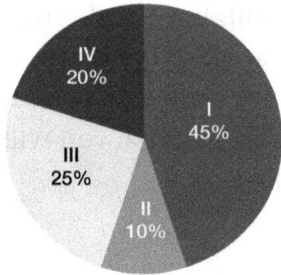

The example shows how much the percentage of time in the four areas mentioned is. It can clearly be seen that the person concerned is rather frustrated and stressed through life.

If we subordinate her eight hours of sleep, then the remaining sixteen hours are distributed as follows:

7,2 hours in category I   →   frustration   45%

1,6 hours in category II   →   stress   10%

4,0 hours in category III   →   stress   25%

3,2 hours in category IV   →   relaxation, joy, success   20%

Once again, remember how much time is spent in an hour per day: If you only watch one less than an hour a day or surf the Internet, that means:

1 hour per day - 365 hours per year - that is 15 full 24-hour-days per year that are additionally available for you. After two years that means one full month FREE!!!

Please write down the following in your "Book of Life":

❯ Calculate in writing how much time you could use more per week.

❯ Calculate the result for one month and for one year and consider the time also for ten years.

❯ What could you do at this time?

❯ How does your life improve when you consciously use this time for your goals?

❯ Write down at least three measures with which you can now spend more time in area IV.

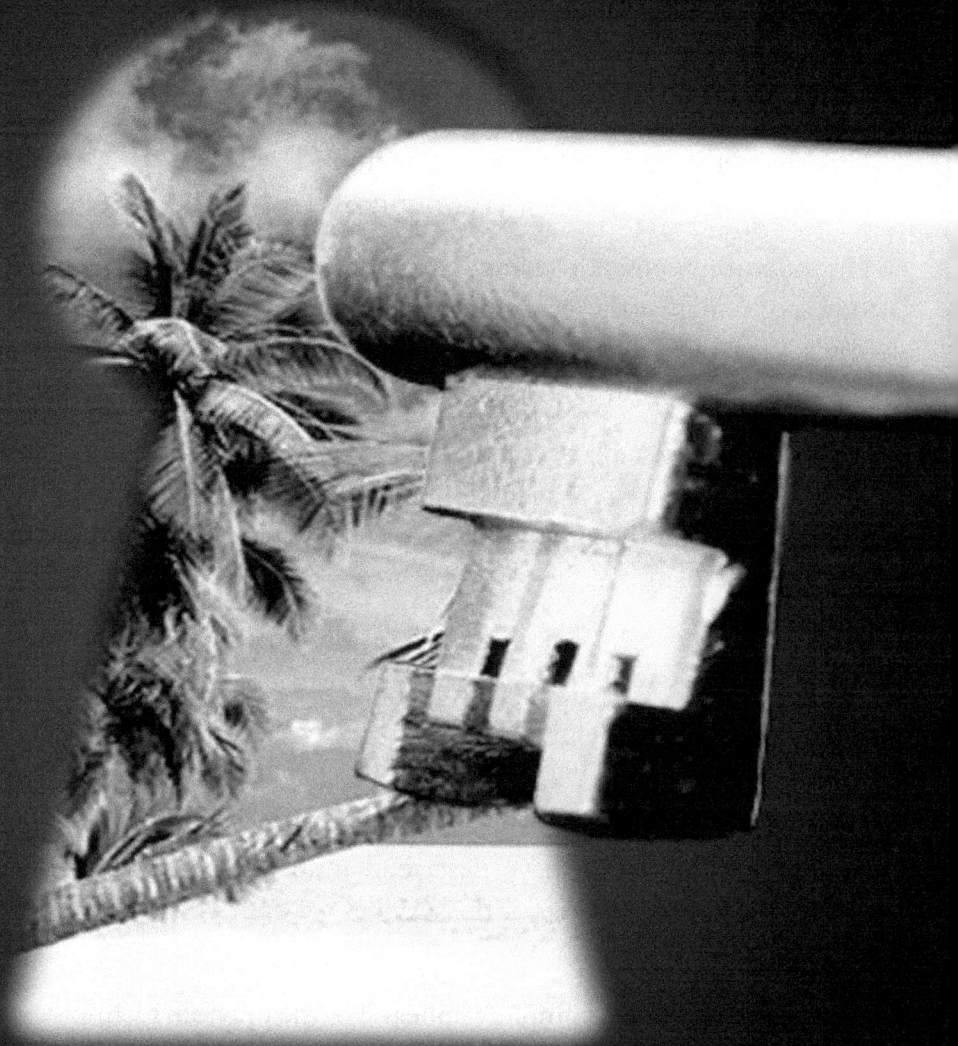

KEY 10

OPTIMIZE YOUR PRODUCTS

Business is innovation and marketing. Peter Drucker

This chapter is designed to help you think about how your products or services could help you achieve your goals.

The common sense of change is that you always come up with new topics, of which at the beginning no one has said anything. As banal as it may sound, but when we change and go new ways, that does not mean that our product, our company or even our fellow human beings change.

We make the best planning for our lives, but it just does not work as desired. We have more time and perhaps more joy, but more money is not yet in sight, even though we have created wonderful scheduling, budget, and resource plans.

What is the reason? What about the products or services we offer? Have we improved as well? If these products lead us to an improvement, we must, of course, also change them. If they were optimal, they would already have ensured that we have more time, more money, more joy.

The whole process of goal-setting, time management, planning, and implementation, as we have described it so far for us humans, can be transferred to the products or the services we offer. Yes, it is even necessary to do that.

In the past few years, a complete upheaval of the previous technology, which has been developed over the years, has been observed. What was unthinkable twenty years ago is now completely normal. Such developments have always existed, but not so in such a short period of time and with such a great spread. I remember well the DIN A4 sheet, filled with holiday reports, which I faxed to my father in the office from Rarotonga, Cook Islands, to Munich in 1992. It took 10 minutes to write this page. Meanwhile, I saw my holiday buddy shrink. 20 US $ cost the life sign from the South Seas. Making calls would have been even more expensive.

Now we have a technique that seems to be able to do everything, even in real time. In the meantime, a high-speed race course was provided to us almost overnight. But many of us still rely on their experience and on their proven car and turn their rounds. They are wondering why others just pass by on the left and right.

Are our products, services, and marketing already high-speed? Has our target group the same needs as a few years ago? Do we know which new or complementary products can result from our know-how due to the expanded technical possibilities? Perhaps we can use our skills to develop products that decouple money from our time.

Your product – A bestseller

> *To sell a product, you need three things:*
>
> *A product, marketing and a technique that allows you to bring information to the customer.*
>
> Frank Kern

Start in reverse order:

1. Technology

In Internet marketing, it is often the opinion that the technology is the all-important thing. There are fantastic platforms and tools that simplify and network everything. Enormous efforts are being made to gather "friends" and "followers", tweet every nonsense, and send one invitation after another to the already annoyed network.

If we simply reduce the supposed power of technology to the areas to which it belongs, then it can be held:

> *"The task of the technology is to deliver the right marketing message via an excellent product to the right market at the right time."* Frank Kern

If you compare it to house construction, technology is about as important as the facade color and the garden fence. Nevertheless, a lot of time and money is invested in this area.

2. Marketing

More important is the right marketing. This still does not make any money. Nevertheless, a great deal of energy and innovation is used here to integrate as many technical systems as possible and to be present everywhere, in order not to miss anything.

> *"Marketing uses the Internet to deliver the right marketing message through an excellent product at the right time to the right people."* Frank Kern

At this point, however, nothing has been sold and nothing has yet been earned. Where is the problem?

First reason: We are almost overwhelmingly overwhelmed by all the possibilities, influences and advice, and we are no longer able to do anything. The reason for this is the lack of concrete goals and effective planning. With such basic principles, we could proceed step by step in a structured way and would always keep an overview.

Second reason: You have not got a product that is so extraordinarily good, will bring great benefits and will greatly change the lives of your customers. It may also be that you have such a product, but have not yet recognized it as such.

3. Outstanding product

A product that is so exceptional that it works like magic for your customers, you can identify with the following statements from your customers:

❯   How much time of my life have I wasted without this product?

❯   How could I live without this product?

You have created an outstanding product if you can effectively lead a customer to a result that results in serious improvements in his life.

On the other hand, the assumption is that you maximize the value for your customers when you provide them with more information. Everyone has enough information, they want results. Nobody wakes up in the night and thinks: I absolutely need a few personality development programs on DVD.

Also the use of "free e-book stories" etc. is questionable, because free of charge always means that we value the value of our performance, our product. This lack of appreciation of our own products transfers to the interested parties. If your product is of great use, you point it out and bring it to the right addressee, then you can confidently demand from the outset as much money as you think fit. However, if you do not meet one of these points, you will not get a lot of money.

Find your answer to the question: "How can my products help my customers to exponentially improve their results?"

Poor people wonder how I can get a euro from a million people. The rich ask themselves, how can I give a million people a value of 10,000 euros and get one percent back? possibly Anthony Robbins

Defining target groups

The best product will not help you if the one you offer it has no use for it. You want to sell a motorbike to someone and show him what a wonderful experience he can have and how wonderful your product will be. He listens to everything and says goodbye to the remark that he does not have a motorbike license. They had a great deal of effort, but they did not succeed because there was no essential requirement for your product to benefit that person.

In order to coordinate a product and the target group, the answers to the following questions are very helpful:

❯ What is my product?

❯ To whom does it benefit?

❯ What is the improvement for my client in everyday life?

❯ Who would like to have this improvement?

> Who can afford the product?

> Where can I find these people?

Go back to goal finding, make a goal finding workshop with your product, it will help you answer the questions. Also, check how your product fits your goals. Is it possible to combine major sales times with your private performances, or are these contradictory? If you sell motorcycles but want to make long journeys in spring and summer in the main sales season, this is in contradiction to each other. Here it would be better to sell winter clothing. Just think about it and agree on your goals and products in certain areas.

You see how similar the process for your personality development and the development process of your product are to each other.

Target groups consist of individual people, and we want to sell something to people and not to the group. I prefer shopping where I feel understood, where I have the impression that they know what I need. For this, the salesman must know what is important to me. Good salespeople recognize this immediately and react to it. With these people, I have the impression that they have known me for years, and I am very quick to trust them. It is then no longer difficult to sell a product when this almost meets my needs.

However, we are not that far, yet. Until there is a personal interview with a prospective customer, there are still a few steps to go. We therefore first define our optimal customer, to whom we would like to deal, as a single person. What the good seller recognizes in conversation, we have to find out in advance about the prospective buyer. Then we can make him feel that we know exactly what is the best solution for him. Now we have won his trust and can show him what advantages the purchase of our product would have for him. But first, we develop the most realistic picture of our ideals.

Sample questions for the definition of our ideal:

> What wishes does your female or male target customer have?

> What are their worries and fears?

> What's their occupation?

> Are they officials or entrepreneurs?

> How much do they earn?

> How do they dress?

> How old are they?

> In what circumstances do they live? House or apartment? Property or for rent? In the city or in the village?

> In which environment do they socially interact? Both business and private?

> Are they single, married, divorced, or widowed?

> Do they have kids?

> What are their hobbies?

> What newspapers do they read?

> How much time do they have?

> What do they like to eat?

> When do they go to bed?

> What are their longings and dreams?

> What makes them special?

What other points are interesting? Where can you find links to your product or service?

From this description, a fictional person develops which you would like to welcome a hundred times a day because this person constantly purchases your products and also rewards them.

If you do not know how to start, ask your best customers. Simply say you want to improve your service and offer. Suitable questions are for example: What would you like as a customer/guest/patient? What do you attach importance to? Ask what he likes and why. From these conversations, you will learn a lot about the individual person, which then you can transfer to others. For many have very similar challenges to master. Be the friend of your customers and help them master these challenges. They will thank you.

Also, check the connections between characteristics of your target group and general surveys (statistics) that might improve your product. An example of this can be found under the heading "sales pyramids".

Sales pyramid

Regardless of what you offer, only about 3% of the people of your target group deal with this topic at the moment when you offer them your product and at the same time have a concrete buying intent.

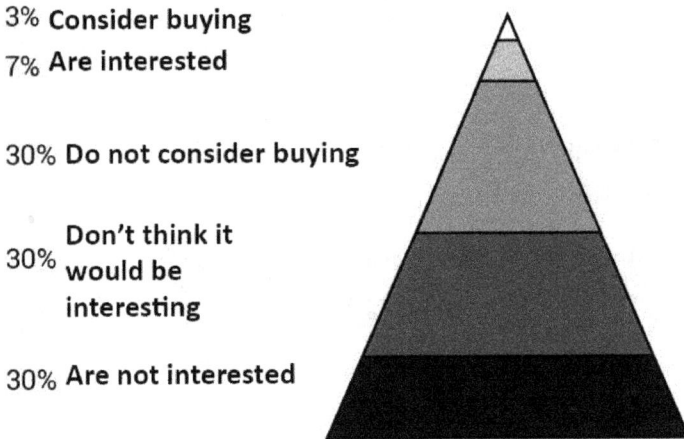

3% **Consider buying**

7% **Are interested**

30% **Do not consider buying**

30% **Don't think it would be interesting**

30% **Are not interested**

source: Chet Holmes, „the ultimate sales machine"

They sell, for example, bicycle Hometrainer:

Three percent of your target group is currently researching about Hometrainer with the intention of buying one. The other 97 percent are only interested in the topic on the edge or not at all. And this is true even if you offer them the best Hometrainer at the best price.

To these three percent, you fight with all other providers. It is about quality, design, equipment, technology, warranty, service and, of course, the price. How can you make your product interesting to the rest of your target group? One way is to go away from the product and to benefit the customer. You need to do a little research, but it's worth it.

Use market data instead of product data to encourage people of your target group to seriously consider whether your product would be interesting to them.

In this example, it could look like this:

You are researching that proves that cardiovascular diseases are the most frequent cause of death in Germany.

41 percent, i.g. 352,700 people died in 2010 due to a cardiovascular disease. Nearly 92 percent of the deceased were at least 65 years old. Source: Federal Statistical Office

Find questions like this one is not too difficult. Then make a reference to your product. It is best to look for a recognized personality in the relevant field and build your argument on your expertise:

"Cycling is the ideal cardiovascular workout." Regular cycling reduces blood pressure and reduces myocardial infarction. Dr. Martin Halle, TU Munich

Not only 3% of your target group, but about 80% feel affected and now think about a purchase. You have not known how valuable your product can actually be for your life. A characteristic of the target group should, of course, be the advanced age in this case.

Your message – a unique opportunity

Now you have defined your product and your target group. You have analysed what characteristics your customer has and how he becomes 150 years old with the help of your product. Furthermore, you have found market data that helps you to combine the characteristics of your product with a benefit for your ideal customer, who was previously unaware of it. What more do you want? Yes, you should tell him, too!

How do you present your offer to your prospective customers so that they can rush your "shop" with enthusiasm to buy your product?

Just think about the lines in front of selling points for concert tickets. Hours before opening, fans are there to make sure that they will get one of the highly coveted tickets. You want to achieve the same with your product, your service, your offer as well.

Now imagine a soccer stadium. It is occupied to the last place. All viewers belong to your target group. You have the opportunity to speak and to amaze the attendees of yourself and your offer in such a way that they become nervous during your speech and move towards the sales stand.

> What would you say if you had three minutes time?

> How would you catch the viewers' attention in such a way that the above sketched scenario takes place??

Think about the TV or radio programs that you are constantly exposed to.

> Which ad makes you pause and watch closely what happens?

> What catches your attention?

> How could you represent this with your product?

Two essential aspects of advertising are to cause pain, then offer a pain-relieving, dreamlike solution in the form of a product. Good ads can do this within sixty seconds.

The girl got lost in the forest, the night is breaking in. Wolves are approaching the child as a howling, shining pairs of eyes watch it. The child is afraid. The scene is gloomy. The girl panics, but fortunately she thinks of her mobile phone with exactly the contract that has the best network coverage. Trembling, she calls her father (fear comes over him). The father sprints out of the office to his helicopter, flies off (he is pure energy). Seconds later he is above the forest. He switches on the thermal sensors and immediately recognizes the contours of his weeping daughter on a forest glade. She is surrounded by wild boars, bears and wolves. The search lights illuminate the forest. Determined to save his little one (he becomes a hero), he places the helicopter hard on the glade, jumps out at the same moment, and takes his daughter into his arm (the savior, the courageous father). Thank you, telephone provider, a thousand thanks! What security you give me. Without this network coverage, my child would have been lost (the telephone company has made me the hero and best father of the world). For which contract will young fathers decide?

A different approach, for products such as baby diapers, usually does not show the smeared diaper and the muffling mom. No, in the purest white, light blue and pink, the sweet little butt is powdered (love) in the sun-drenched bathroom (purity, the dream of all mothers) and wrapped in the comfortably warm, soft and leak-safe diaper (suggesting security against unpleasant situations for the mommy), Immediately there is an intimate embrace of mom and baby (mama, you're the best, the baby wants to say, and the mommy submits the praise subconsciously to the nappy). Mom quickly takes the child and dresses it for the mommy-baby meeting, where she reports about the new diaper. The girlfriends are also enthusiastic and thank the mommy warmly for the good tip (Mama also thinks about the well-being of others and receives a praise. Who thanks her otherwise? Who gives her security? Who makes her baby happy and especially quiet for a couple of minutes? Thank you, dear diaper producer!). At the end of the commercial, it is mentioned that the diaper in the large pack for the special price (more for less money) is only available today and tomorrow (demand for action with time pressure). This means happiness, praise and joy in large format at a reduced price. Give them to me right now!

> Could you now step onto the stage and present your product perfectly and convincingly?

> Could your back-office employees do so?

> Could your sales representatives do so?

> Do your flyers, your brochures and your website tell the same story?

Google, Facebook and Co

What would you do if your products were placed at the top pages of Google?

Here are a few thoughts:

What does Google want? – To make money, of course. But they must remain market leaders. How do they do that? – With the help of the quality of the search results.

You and I, we're just looking at Google as long as we find what really interests us.

Are we looking for expert advice or superficial talk?

Where do you feel better advised – at the supermarket or at the retailer? If the retailer is also a first-class expert and has long been in business, then you trust him and buy there.

Google & Co think and act in their ranking the same way. In addition, Google asks if there is something to be found about his friends and foes. Facebook or Youtube are very popular. If you are to be found there as well, this will strengthen the good impression on Google, and your site will increase in placement. Of course, the search engines recognizes whether your address is listed on other sites and whether they are clicked on there, too. They also check whether it is a page that matches your activity, and how often the page is frequented.

It is also important that your page is up-to-date. It is precisely when and how often you make changes. These and certainly some other routines examine the search engines and thereby form their judgment on your page. This judgment is reflected in the placement of the search results.

An important point is also the search terms, because they determine under which terms your page can be found. Because you can't tell the millions of people out there what they're looking for, just turn the tables. Find out which terms the people type into Google to find something similar to your topic. For this, Google even offers tools that tell you exactly what terms were searched for, how many results were obtained, and what other terms were searched for in this context. The tool is called Google AdWords (and is of course easy to be googled). There is still a whole lot of information on SEO - Search Engine Optimization, which means measures that improve the searchability of your site through search engines. But that would go beyond the scope of this book.

If you want the search engines to help you, first help them to recognize your value based on the structure and content of your website!

A short checklist for your website:

> Are you an expert in your field with your subjects, headlines, pictures, texts, videos, links, etc. - or are you suggestive of having a "hawkers' tray"?

> Is your topic included in your domain name? If you are your own topic, then include your name in the domain.

> Do you know what your target group is googling, and are these search terms in your texts and headings available?

> Do you regularly add and update your content?

> Is the link to your website on other, qualified websites?

There are many other points and topics that make sense regarding the ranking. It is essential that you develop your web presence in a calculated and structured manner. You can also turn it into a project, to a product that you further improve goal-oriented.

Email autoresponder – automate your processes!

What do get from having first position on Google, when people come to your homepage, there also find what they are looking for, but then they don't buy anything ... They come and go and leave only traces in the web analytics (programs with which you can analyze the traffic on your site). You can determine whether a few visitors are buying a lot, or if a lot of visitors do not buy anything. On the basis of this knowledge, you can then start "Troubleshooting". Many visitors and few sales speak for your search engine optimization and against your product. Few visitors, however, who buy a lot, means the opposite. In this case, it would be good to bring more potential customers to your site.

The direct comparability between visit and sale exists, of course, only if you operate an onlineshop. Nevertheless, it is important in any case to be informed about the visitor numbers. You can use this information to identify trends.

On average, an interested buyer must contact you about 7-10 times to buy a product or service.

How do you do that? The buyer is now in front of your shop window. Figuratively, he stands in front of your restaurant in a beautiful piazza and reads the menu.

In the Mediterranean region, a good waiter would approach you now. Where do you come from, how do you like our city? At the same time, while you are still undecided, he will give you a small, cool drink with a straw, as a gift, of course. With the glass in your hand you are forced to stay a little longer. The straw prevents you from pouring it down in two seconds. He uses this time to describe his offers in the most beautiful colors. He will show you the best table and will calm you with moderate prices.

On the Internet, you do not have the opportunity to clarify the situation by a short conversation.

> So, who is going to pick up the interested person on your website?

> Who approaches him, before he moves on?

If the temptation is big and the risk is low - as in the case of the Italian waiter - there are good ways to persuade the prospective buyer to stay so that he can receive more offers. You will need his name and e-mail address.

The email follow-up responder is a stand-alone e-mail management program, which also provides a form for submitting (as you know it from the newsletter programs). The visitors can enter their name and e-mail address in these blank fields. With this data, you have the possibility, within the framework of the legal requirements, to provide the interested party with further information.

Briefly something about the technical aspect. After the data is entered, the responder automatically sends a security query, the so-called double opt-in routine, to the registered e-mail address. The receipt of this confirmation mail must be confirmed by clicking on the link contained. This is an abuse protection that ensures that no third party uses third party e-mail addresses. Before registering, you must inform the visitor in accordance with the legal data protection guidelines that this information is free of charge, non-binding and can be canceled at any time. Of course, you also declare that you will not pass on the data to third parties. In any case, check the current legal situation before using the system.

It is the only way to get to the visitors in the future in an active and time-optimized manner and to bring them benefits in the form of your offers.

The records are documented and stored by the responder system. Another advantage is the personalized sending of e-mails. This means that each recipient is personally addressed with his or her name. The system allows you to send information automatically, even with dates. The approach by name creates trust and the automation leads to great time efficiency, especially in customer care.

Many websites now offer newsletters, but only a few of them have information that really brings something to the potential customer or even inspires him and helps to solve his problem.

Take advantage of this opportunity and the trust you have already shown. You now have the opportunity to communicate with your future customer with very little time, establish a trust relationship and finally establish a business relationship with him. Here comes the real challenge separating the wheat from the chaff.

Back to the Italian. Imagine you are sitting at your table now, waiting and waiting, and nothing happens. No waiter, no menu. Honestly, this makes me very angry, and since I am an impatient person, I leave after a short period of time. I will definitely not go back to this place. I will not recommend it.

I was attracted, but then nothing was delivered to further build trust and create the foundations for a successful transaction.

Why is this often the case with newsletters? Either none will be delivered, or there are so many newsletters with up to 99% useless information, so that one does not look at them anyway and is rather annoyed. The main reason is inadequate planning. At least for half a year, better for a whole year in advance, the planning should bring up which offers and information are interesting. That is too much planning? But if you have a few hours to think about topics and content twice a year with your employees (and perhaps with some of your existing customers), then you have certainly 12 topics that you can distribute throughout the year. This compressed time investment saves you not only a lot of time but also nerves compared to monthly individual actions. It reduces the pressure, now necessarily having to send something. Again, change "important and urgent" into "important, but not urgent". This means less stress.

You can specify the time of shipment in advance for all mails. This allows you to take care of vacation periods, holidays, special events, etc. In the ideal case, certain events can even be used to enhance your information.

With this method, you have a contact with your prospective customers every month. You can add additional mail or modify existing ones at any time.

However, since the visitors are not all registered in January, the responder can be set up in such a way that the information already sent in the current year is forwarded at fixed intervals. The normal sequence is then adopted. Thus, no one escapes information. However, you should make sure that Easter greetings are not sent on Christmas. This means that the contents should be kept neutral in time.

Basically, everything can be done, depending on the provider. It is a very fine thing, with which you can save a lot of time incredibly simple and cost-saving. Through building up trust and your first-class products, you can turn your prospects into actual customers.

A further advantage of the information mails is that they can easily be forwarded. This way, your prospects and customers distribute your information at the click of a mouse. It is similar to the site recommendation with social media, but I think it is much more personal.

The topics discussed above are meant to give you a few thought-provoking insights and points-of-view to consider your existing products and marketing in terms of new technical possibilities.

Could your knowledge also be a product?

You have collected so much experience in your field, thought so intensively about it, and developed so many solutions. Of course, you are now benefiting from it in your daily work. Your customers do that, too. But could you not package this knowledge differently and sell it as a stand-alone product? Of course, it is not advisable to deliver the own know-how to the competition free of charge. Just think for whom your experience and insights are useful. Who would say, "Wow, he has a clue. If I need something in this area, then I can ask him." ?

Think about whether you want to use your knowledge to develop and sell an independent information or education product.

The quality of your products

As I said, I am not a friend of "Free E-Book" etc., although here is often important and good information to be found. But somehow, these things give me the subliminal feeling that they are not worth anything. Moreover, it is a question of attitude. If I have an outstanding product or exclusive knowledge, then it is allowed to and should also cost something.

If a craftsman bores you a hole in the wall, he doesn't do it free, just to prove he can, right? When you go to the doctor or lawyer, you know that you will get a bill as soon as you say "Greetings".

Be aware of how your product improves your customer's life. What benefits does it have and what dangers does it protect from? How it minimizes his risk and how long he can use it. Then write down a sum that would be worth it to you. This is your price.

You may not be able to achieve this amount in competition, but it is extremely important for you and your subconscious mind to know the true value. Because then you quickly lose the pleasure of price reductions and dumping prices, and you notice the opposite. The interested parties must decide between cheap goods and first-class quality including service. In support of the purchase decision, you may mention the "Law of the Economy" by John Ruskin towards your customers.

> „There is nothing in the world that some man cannot make a little worse and sell a little cheaper, and he who considers price only is that man's lawful prey.
>
> It is unwise to pay too much, but it is even worse to pay too little. If you pay too much, you will lose some money, that's all. If on the other hand, you pay too little, you sometimes lose everything, since the purchased item can't fulfill the task assigned to it.
>
> The law of the economy prohibits a lot of value for little money. If you take the lowest bid, you need to calculate something additionally for the risk. And if you do, you'll have enough money to pay for something better. "Ruskin

From marketing to sales

In the following, the most important points on marketing and sales are summarized with new media. Check again which of the above points still offer you a potential for improvement.Describe the benefits of your product to the customer. Show the prospective customer the benefits of your product by answering the following questions:

> How does it improve his life, the life of his family or of his friends?

> How will he experience appreciation and praise if he uses your product?

> What dangers does it keep away from him?

> How long can he use it?

> What risk does he have to fall "flat on his face" with the product?

> How can he afford it?

> What does he have to do to get it?

If you have answered these questions and have defined your target group exactly, then you should look for these people. Or in other words:

Make it easy for people to find you.

Generate more contacts

This can be done through blogs, websites, search engine optimization, radio, PR measures, letters, mailings, social media, videos, exhibitions, crossover marketing, events, calls. Of course, everything within the scope of the permitted possibilities and with style.

> With what measures do you win how many contacts per week?

> How many contacts are your goal and why?

> What do you have to optimize in order to achieve that?

Improve your sales processes

If you have gained more contacts, you often need personal appointments. Not all products are sold online. The Internet is an excellent tool in many areas, but it is not always enough.

> Make more appointments with decision-makers,

> Increase the number of follow-up appointments for product presentation and sales.

Also, create a small overview of the contacts you had until someone bought your product. This clearly shows where you are strongest and where you are working efficiently and profitably. This means that you can see if, for example, you make 80% of your initial contact sales and use 20% of your time. This would mean you use 80% of your time on second and third contacts that will bring you only the remaining 20% of sales.

This allows you to see very quickly where time and profit potentials lie and have the chance to better allocate your time. If your table looks similar to the one in the example, then you should invest considerably more time into your first contacts. For this, you can omit third-party contacts, which can only make a loss.

You can also use this time for improvements in the service and customer support and thus generate more after-sales with little effort.

In addition, you have time to ask for referrals. And you can make sure that they are placed and made public. This in turn brings more attention, which leads to more initial contacts etc. You see, if you recognize where you lose time, you can also make improvements without having to work 28 hours a day.

> *If you recognize where you lose time you can also make improvements.*

Make more of your product

You have eliminated a few "time-eaters" and improved your service. Now you can also offer the optimized service in addition. For example, in the framework of an exclusive membership with special service offers, which are otherwise not available or only for a lot of money. Improve your offer continuously and show the benefit to the customer. Use this to support your argumentation as well as your statements "to prove".

Service and guarantee assurances are very good arguments for canceling your discounts and price reductions. Prices can also easily be justified by product improvements.

Lead your customers and interested persons

Show your customers and prospects the next steps. These are quite trivial things which are the most important.

Make it easy for them to contact you if they have questions.

> Make it easy for them to buy the products with telling them, where they are directly available.

> What payment methods can they use and how quickly do they get their money back if they are not satisfied?

> Suggest solutions about how easily your product can be integrated in their lives.

> Think through the sequence, until the time when your customers – full of joy –have improved their life with the new product.

> Think about what else you could do good and offer it.

In short

> Create a product that improves the lives of your customers.

> Clarify for whom (target group) it is most beneficial and explain why. (Sales pyramid).

> Generate new contacts, use technology to turn marketing into profit.

> Turn your contacts and prospects into clients by showing the benefits of your offers.

> Inspire your customers with more performance than they would expect.

> Provide supplementary services that fit well with your offer.

> Increase the follow-up frequency, but listen in time before it becomes obtrusive and embarrassing.

> Keep the customer relationship up longer, even if no purchases are made.

> Stay motivated in the case of cancellations and complaints and try to figure out the reasons. This is a gold mine for further optimization.

> Reactivate old customers, but pay attention to the legal situation.

> Share the positive experiences of your customers with your products by video and written references.

> Show your customers the next steps.

Summary

We have optimized our product and planned it well. We know what we want and why we want it. We have also found time reserves in which we can realize our plans. Everything is wonderful and very important (but hopefully not urgent, yet). Now we only have to trust ourselves to do it.

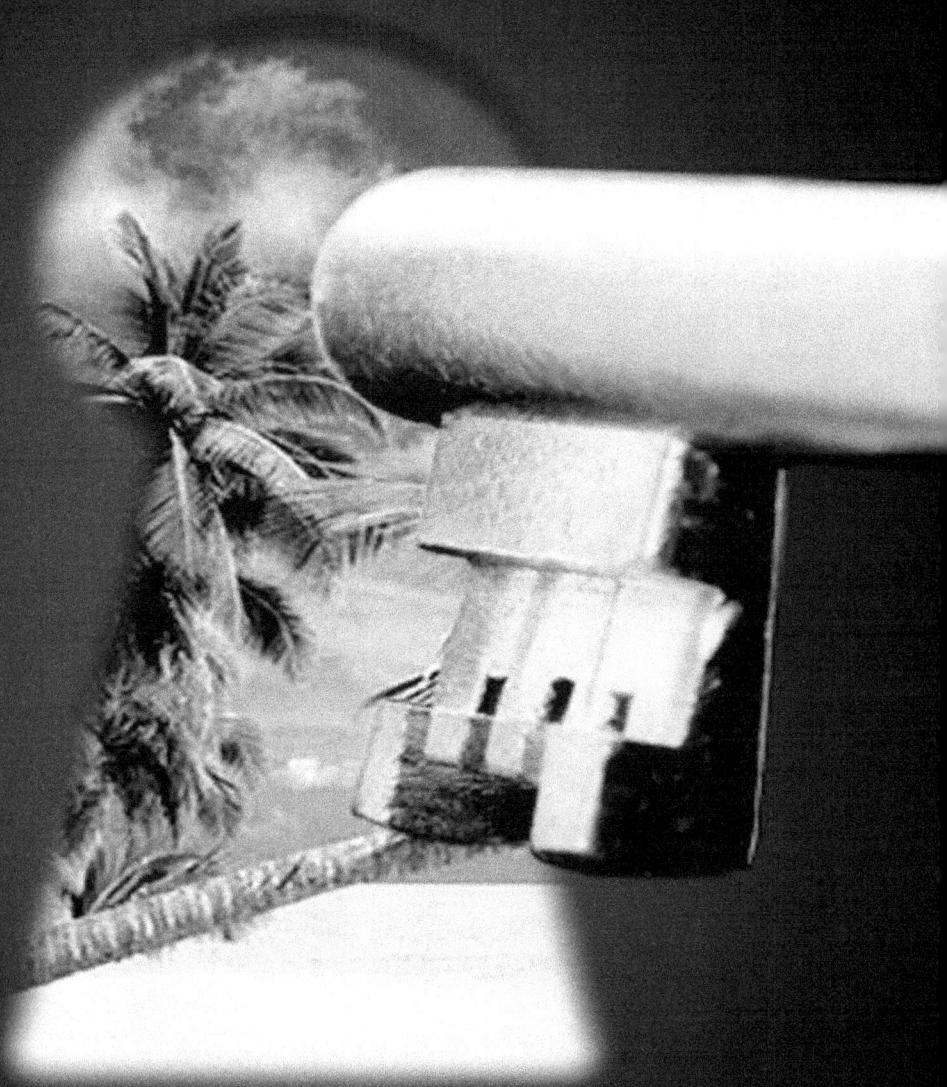

KEY 11

SET THE RIGHT FOCUS

Be – self – confident

If we have experienced more often in our lives that we can't reach our goals with our abilities, we can't develop stable self-esteem. As a result, we suffer from mood swings. We are particularly nervous when an important appointment, a test or a performance is due. Sometimes we even get frightened and become obnoxious towards ourselves and others. Hypersensitivity, nervousness, inner unrest, and irritability are a sign of a lack of self-confidence.

> *We build up self-confidence only when we are convinced of ourselves and our abilities. We must be convinced that our skills help us achieve our goals (self-efficacy). The more positive experiences we make, the more stable our self-confidence becomes.*

A good self-confidence can be recognized by the following features:

> We are self-confident, if we know our goal exactly and are absolutely focused on it.

> If we know exactly what we are doing, we can also assess how much physical and mental strength and endurance is necessary. Accordingly, we can prepare ourselves and largely mitigate this uncertainty. So, we are also very stable here and feel safe.

> If we know what we want and are certain of our strength, there are also people who can give us reassurance. They give us honest, constructive support, but also qualified criticism.

What are we mostly focusing on? The beautiful and good things in our life, that is almost done by itself? Or do we let ourselves be caught by what is just not working? Do we, in order to solve this "detail", become increasingly stressed? Do we often forget all the other beautiful things that were around us or in our past?

We will get what we focus on. The challenge is to actually focus on the point you want to achieve. Often, however, we focus on the point that we just do not want to meet, just to be sure that we don't have to deal with them.

> *Our whole education is designed to avoid harm and*
> *not to solve the problem.*

Don't get up there, you will fall down! Do not do this, or something will happen! Go away, from that or you'll hurt yourself! – These sentences are very popular on playgrounds. Unfortunately, they often lead to the opposite result. The children, and later also the adults, do not concentrate on holding, but on the non-dropping. When the child actually falls down, the sentence immediately follows: "I told you!". This again confirms the correctness of the warning. And so, we begin to believe and learn from an early age on to focus on the danger.

We are taught to focus on the problem that needs to be addressed. In doing so, we focus on the "danger site" with the utmost precision. That is our problem!

I can remember how I got new skis as a teenager. It was a nice, sunny day, and I burned the stage. The ski ran perfectly. There was actually a stone lying around in the middle of the slopes. I looked at it and thought:

"I'm not going to take it" I also looked at the snow buckle on the slope, looked at the stone again, considered whether I should go left or right, look and .... craack! Direct hit and a nice scratch in the covering. 'You can't be that stupid,' was my first thought.

I felt the same way on other occasions. It annoyed me very much, but I had no idea why this happened again and again. Until a friend from the BMW racing team told me that the racing drivers are trained to look at the gap as soon as they get skidding. They exercise to turn the head abruptly in the direction of the gap, the way out, in order to turn. Supposedly, our subconsciousness engages and does what it always does: focus on that

"Goal". In the good as well as the bad (because it can't think on its own).

When the captain roars down the bridge over the voice tube: "Full power ahead!", The heaters in the lower floor heat up, confidently and without a look outside. It is unfortunate if the captain has focused on a rock that he wants to avoid ...

I find these examples very memorable, and so I tell you about them, even though it is badly done in a book. You must first read what is to be done, and then you know the "trick" already. So, try it with friends or acquaintances. Describe the exercise as follows:

Look around in the room you are in. Try to remember everything that is green or blue. Imagine things. Maybe a picture on the wall, the carpet floor or the vase in the showcase. No matter, you'll notice anything green or blue. This includes a book or the magazine, which mainly uses these colors. Now close your eyes, go through the things you saw with your mind's eye, and tell me now - while you keep your eyes further closed: What things in this area are brown?

You will find that most people do not remember a single brown object (unless the room is very familiar to the test persons). This example makes it clear that we only perceive what we are aware of. And we do that by focusing on it.

Relaxation develops through the right focus

I assert that there is not a single situation in life where we would not be able to find anything bad about it and which gets us upset. Then it is easy for us to be in a bad mood. Of course, we also find support through news about injustices and fraud. This makes it even easier to focus further on the crisis, thus even coming into the crisis and remaining there.

In most cases, it is only small things that we are upset about, but we are constantly looking for them and they are shown to us from all sides. These little "troublemakers" are constantly gnawing at us. They are like the little beetles that bring down a large oak tree after surviving every storm, war, and tree house for two hundred years.

Relaxation and joy in life come when we focus on what really means something to us. At the same time, it is necessary to largely eliminate the "disturbance of the disturbance" and to estimate its status as realistically as possible.

Those who do not do this are constantly in the reaction to other people and other things. They live in a constant distraction, which leads them to reach their goals (which they don't always know) more and more rarely. This makes them even more frustrated, they achieve even less, get into greater stress, and the anger about God and the world escalates.

In order to distract themselves again, they are looking for and finding things that offer a supposed relaxation in the short term. Very popular here is watching TV in combination with two or three beers and a few potato chips "full of energy" (salty, fat). The joy is great, because here they find confirmation that their catastrophic situation is not dependent on them, but on the crises, and therefore on the mighty ones in the world. There is sufficient evidence on all channels.

Since this is not enough to completely neglect their own focus, they also follow the demands, interests and wishes of others. Because the - sometimes badly interrupted film - is very appealing. The makers of these commercials have done their homework with regard to target group definition. Thus, they draw attention to offers that coincide with their taste and needs. They promise solutions without which they most likely can't make it beyond next week. They buy the products they didn't even know yesterday, and are thus financially a step further away from their real life plans ...

Set focus and keep it

We've seen what happens when we focus on the wrong goal. We look at the stone to determine the distance, so we can make it past the stone. - Not only the last sentence is difficult to understand, but also the process. What does our unconscious mind think when it obviously can't see anything? It thinks, "I'll just aim for the direction he looks at and to what he's always thinking about, to the stone."

Wouldn't it be easier to look at the gap, on the whole wide, white slope that provides so much space? A quick glance at the stone would have been enough to recognize it and change the direction. I would, without realizing it, pass the stone by far. Because this is the reversal function: a small warning and positioning by the brain, and the subconscious has saved the position as a danger and does not try to get to this danger as close as possible. When the eyes then focus on the target, there is no longer any danger. We will discuss this behavior in the chapter "Success is a process / Solution finding".

What possibilities are there now to reprogram our brain so that it looks at the solution and not at the problem? A good way to support that are target collages.

Goal collages – Focus support in good and bad times

We had already discussed the visual fixation of your goals in the chapter on goal-setting. Since our subconscious mind is very important for the achievement of our goals, and this subconscious mind is oriented towards images, we come back to the importance of collages.

Collages or target collages are images and slogans of our goals and dreams that we stick to a large clay cardboard. The more emotionally these images and sentences vibrate within us, the better is their effect on us.

The goals should be great. It is a pleasure for us to look at them. And we should feel fully integrated into the stories that trigger the images in us. We smell the scent, feel the warmth, hear the voices and noises. We feel the future as if it were already a reality. This is the key point: the goal is always a feeling we would like to have. This feeling is to be found in the day room. "I feel the warm sand and turquoise water in the lagoon, I hear the waves breaking out on the reef and feel one with the elements. I lie on the beach, while the children dive in the lagoon ... "

I feel well, I have arrived and am deeply relaxed. I want to always feel like that, it can't always be bad.

To get into this mode more easily, I look for fantastic pictures, print them out and stick them on a large piece of cardboard. It is enough to look at my goals, the emotions and the reasons.

No matter in what mood we are, the pictures help us to focus on our goals. The more emotional, the better. This applies to all areas of life. You should always look carefully at the pictures and enter the respective scene.

With that, you help your brain to focus on your goals. Because the focus, the view, is where we are headed. In the course of time, you can feel the joy of watching certain aspects. It is easy to fall into short day dreams. These are the areas where you feel comfortable and where you can be sure that this goal is a deep-rooted longing. You have taken the right path.

A South Sea trip with the whole family is a costly and time-consuming project. Maybe you need another job. One in which you can blossom, to bring brilliant achievements and consequently earn so much money and have so much free time that the trip becomes possible. This can be a long and difficult path. This is a path where you often have doubts and maybe even want to give up. At times, you no longer believe it, but it is now on your collage, and you see and feel the goal and know the reasons why you need to achieve that goal.

You go on and on and on again to master one challenge after another. Every passing challenge is a change towards your goals.

How these changes look, surprised again and again. Often, a lot of ballast is left on the track, which you can no longer drag around. It is a ride up and down between high-mindedness and self-doubt, in which your collage always helps you to get out of the thought carousel. Then it is the navigation system to your goals.

In addition, get out into the fresh air, run and power yourself out, with the images and feelings of your wonderful future in your head. If now confidence and the feeling of strength and energy are developed, then you are on the right track.

With the collage, you have a guide during a tough period, a map you can always orient yourself on. The prerequisite, however, is that you start, reduce the distraction attempts from the outside (other people and supposedly important, irreversible things) and from within (your own patterns and fears) and correct your course in case of deviations. You can find out how to do this in the chapter "Distractions".

> *The goal is always a feeling we would like to have.*
> *This feeling is to feel as if it is already real in the*
> *day dream.*

KEY 12

CONTROL OF SPEECH – OF THOUGHTS AND WORDS

What are words and how do they work?

Words have a great effect on us. Although they are only pressure waves transmitted via the air, they are absorbed by the eardrum as vibration, converted into bioelectrical signals and processed by the brain. At this point, the impulses meet interpretation, conditioning and experience from the past. This creates a feeling – good or bad. It does not matter if the information is correct or wrong, whether it applies to us or not. There is a certain feeling created in us, quite automatically, we can do almost nothing against it.

Tell a lady how pretty she looks today. – If you feel like it's a straight lie, and it doesn't want to come out of your mouth, just praise her kind, sympathetic personality. What effect do you think these sound waves have? If it sounds honest, you'll conjure a radiant smile on the lady's face. If you are a lady, compliment a man and tell him what a gentleman he is. If you feel this as a lie, try it with a positive remark about his car, for us men that's usually enough.

Everyone is happy about compliments and reacts to them – even if not immediately. For me it would probably come to a small delay until the joy becomes really visible, since I first have to overcome my pattern to look serious, before I am heartily pleased with a compliment and thereby relax my gaze.

If, on the other hand, you send out sound waves that might make you seem unsympathetic, selfish, making the opposite feel like a stupid goat or stupid dog, the facial features will solidify and the following conversation will most likely not be very successful

Try it out, test a few words that are honest and not imposed.

Do not exaggerate, however, like the people who constantly smile and act super friendly. Those who are hardly able to catch up with enthusiasm when they see you. If, as you look at the grinning face, your neck-hairs are set up and you think: "Creep," then something is wrong with the joy, and your sense makes you feel that. But if it is the same heartfelt joy as that of your children, when they walk towards you with joy, then it is wonderful.

A few words from the heart (even if they are not quite right) do in any case well and everyone feels better. They make people more open. This results in good discussions and new possibilities, whether private or business.

I was once with a female architect in the district administration. The person responsible for authorizing the border was regarded as old-fashioned and very retracted. We were thinking back and forth about how we could convince the civil servant just before retirement to approve our planning. We did not bring it to a safe strategy, so we went into the meeting with mixed feelings. A stern look at two young people, you could see on the mans' face that he thought, 'What do you want here?'. But after the "Greetings" the architect asked: "How are you?" You won't believe how the facial features of the man changed. The tension, the prejudices against us, were gone. A short sentence, which shows interest in the opposite, often has a great effect. With pleasure, he gave us all that we wanted, and gave us even a few good hints about how to make it even better. This is the effect of words on others - how do you think your own words will affect you first?

The power of thoughts and words about ourselves

For years, I've been telling myself I wasn't good enough, and I was frustrated not to know everything I could have learned in so many aspects. A few years ago, a good friend made me aware of this, which of course is logical, but was not internalized: "You will never know everything, even if you turn 3,000 years old."

The challenge is to not always persuade ourselves that we are not good enough, which leads to us being in a bad mood.

The approach is as described in the chapter "Important is relative": we have to ask more closely what our thoughts and words actually mean. The statement: "I am not good enough" is relative. Not good enough for what? For whom? In which situation? When I thought about these questions, I realized that it was mostly only small aspects in which I had felt, thought, and talked that way. In addition, it was often aspects that interested me only marginally and about which I could not know much.

My realization, then, was to only consider myself needed where I really had something to say and where I wanted to say something. My high demands towards myself changed in a way I no longer believed I had to know everything, but wanted to be curious to supply my general knowledge and consolidate it. I don't mind not being an expert everywhere.

Through this change of my point of view, I changed my mind and consequently my words and feelings towards myself. This, in turn, increased my satisfaction with myself and passed on to my success.

My self-confidence was reduced to my focus on a few areas of knowledge that suited me. As a result, my thoughts, my expression, and my charisma improved.

Accusations to others or to oneself lead to bad feelings, and we should not do that. Let us ask ourselves again what we want, and in what areas we want it.

Do we want to feel sorry for ourselves and think badly of ourselves? Or do we want to be successful?

If you choose the latter, word and thought control are valuable tools in everyday life.

The only question is how we do it. We do not actually even notice what we are talking about all day and what we think. If one can believe in various investigations, then the human being thinks about 60,000 – 80,000 thoughts every day. Only about 3 – 5% are positive, building up thoughts. The remaining are negative thoughts of concern, of doubt as well as neutral thoughts. Fueled by alleged misunderstandings and self-doubt, supported by bad news on television and radio, encouraged by stress at work. What do you think is always happening within ourselves when we are constantly talking to ourselves and thinking about ourselves? I've been doing this for years and ruined my mood continuously.

Do we want to feel sorry for ourselves or do we want to be successful?

Being aware of your own words

Two very decisive words, to which we should be aware of, are: "I am". How often do we say about ourselves: "I am tired, I am burned out, I am angry, etc."

For a car it would be clear, could a car speak, it would not say of itself: I'm blue, I'm rusty, I'm fast. The car says I am a car, I have a blue paint, the paint on the right fender is peeling off, and the sheet is rusting at this point. How would you feel if someone were saying about your car: "Your car is rusty!" They would probably correct it and point out that on the front fender on the right, there is a small rusty spot, but you will soon get rid of it.

With the car, we pay close attention to the fact that our car is not called a "rusty box". As far as our expression is concerned, we are grossly negligent. After all, we were trained for years, and as a baby we were constantly hearing these words: "Now you are tired, now you are sad, now you are good."

I am Christian, and that describes the state of being, it says who I am. When I say,

"I am angry," I believe, because of my conditioning, to be annoyed. This is the fatal thing: we still believe in it and we also say it in full emotions. These are the best prerequisites to remember properly our subconscious mind. It wants to realize the state we have expressed and thought as well as possible, and does everything to bring us into this state and to hold it there.

It would be correct to say, for example, that "the result of this discussion does not correspond to my ideas and is annoying me for this and that reason".

It sounds admittedly very swollen, but we immediately gain a distance from the problem and can consider it "neutral", assess it and look for solutions. We do not project our anger at ourselves, but we express clearly what is actually the reason for our annoyance.

The result of this review is the reason for our annoyance. We can isolate and edit the meeting result. We can look for the cause of the unwanted result and take care of this detail. We do not have to make ourselves brittle by speaking badly of a generalized choice of words.

With "I am" we relate everything to our whole being. This is often not the case, and above all: it is only true in the rarest cases. Instead of "I'm angry," it is better to say and to think: "The dog of my neighbor yesterday annoyed me again because he is constantly peeing at our garden fence." Now you have found the culprit. This allows you to influence the dog. For example, you could talk to a dog owner about a solution.

If you pay attention to the words "I am" for a few days, you will be so sensitive to them that you always notice when you use them. This allows you to choose the next word carefully. Furthermore, please check as frequently as possible what causes an irritation or other undesirable condition and how often that actually occurs. Here are words like "always", "all the time", "continuous" etc. the signal generators. Even if you initially say: "I'm so mad", you can still add "for the next 30 seconds". This is a time limit for your condition, which is manageable. After this period of time you and your subconscious mind no longer need to worry about it.

When I began to track words and phrases like "always", "all the time", "everything is …", "everyone is …", "I am …" and immediately questioned them, that was the beginning of a whole new language. And that had a big impact on my state of mind. I recognized more and more that I wasn't meant as a whole being, but everything had a cause to be recognized and removed. This I have made myself aware of, and I was always feeling better afterwards.

When I questioned the phrase "everything is bad", it turned out that in reality very few things were bad. They were not "always" like this, but only at few times and usually only for a short period.

The moment I "catch" one of these words or one of these thoughts, I formulate them and leave the new sentence "free" again. For example, I'm not saying "I'm tired," but I am reducing this condition to the actual window of time and looking for the reason for my fatigue, describe it, and try to correct the cause.

Instead of saying, "Today I'm tired," it leads to a more comfortable condition, as follows: "The three beers and the short night are the reason that today it was difficult to get out of bed and fit". You immediately recognize the cause and can find a simple solution. Drink less beer and sleep more. I know it is unfamiliar and sounds silly at first, but at least try it out in your self-talk.

There, nobody can hear you and you can be honest with yourself. At the very latest, if you can smile at your causes and their description, this language and the new way of formulating thoughts will be fun to you. Because no longer are you to blame for everything, but the small indispositions that are usually easy to fix.

My mood was slowly improving, and I was able to get out of the deep phase very quickly. I managed to change my focus by simple means. Not because I wanted and forced myself, but because everything else was simply not tenable. It was absurd to talk myself down all day because of one minute and to feel bad. My self-esteem rose and it also helped me defuse "attacks" from the outside because I knew that what was attacked was not me, but only a behavior of mine that was now unpleasant for the "attacker". I could more and more react almost emotionally, because I felt not affected.

> Is it in fact always? – How many minutes per day objectively?

> Is it really everyone? – Who is it objectively?

> The whole time? So, 24/7/365?

> ❯ Is everything bad? – What is really bad? Even the laughter of your children, the fresh water, the warm bed and the good food?

About Buddha it was said that he was not to be worked up, no matter how he was challenged or insulted. A man came from far away. He wanted to challenge Buddha. He tried everything to get him ruffled, and finally insulted him for the worst. Buddha did not say a word and stood still. When the man had tried everything, Buddha asked him the following:

"If someone gives you a present and you do not accept it, then who owns the gift?" The man replied, "The one who brought it." Buddha said, "This is right". The man recognized the message of the answer. He apologized to Buddha and moved on ashamed.

If you do not accept verbal abuse and reproaches, they can't harm you. Unless they are justified in certain respects. Then it is up to you to create them out of the world and to develop a step further. So you have developed a broad basis for healthy self-awareness. By raising awareness of your thoughts and words, you can strengthen yourself and therefore also be self-confident towards others.

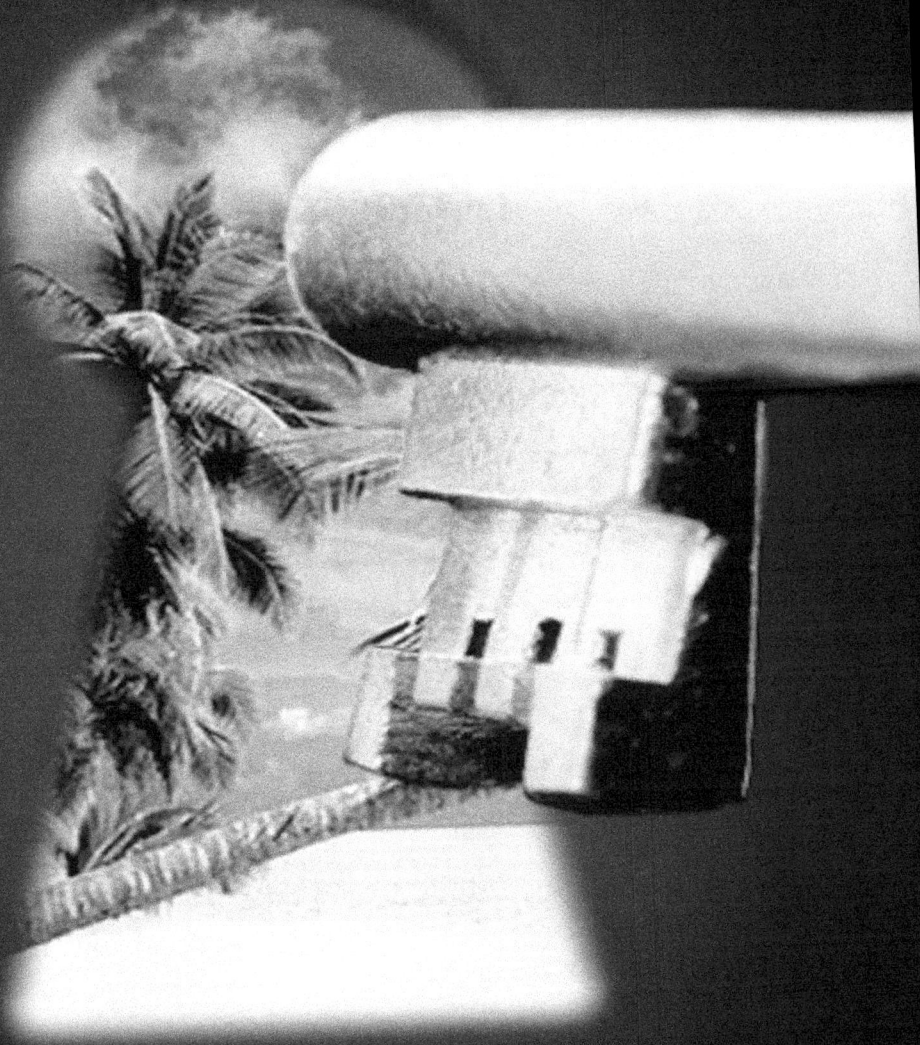

KEY 13

A GOOD PHYSICAL CONDITION

Posture

> *Health is not only the absence of illness, but also a*
> *positive feeling of life, which can be experienced with*
> *joy and with the help of one's own, resilient body.*

Self-awareness is nourished by this vitality, which is dependent on fitness and physical condition.

How does a person move who has no self-confidence?

How would you describe this person?

Try to figure it out, stand up, your feet slightly turned inwards, the shoulders hanging downwards, the upper body slightly overhanging, the head lowered, the corners of the mouth downwards and a look like the proverbial "puddled poodle". For this, the breathing is quite flat. Put the book aside for a moment and walk a few steps through the room. Watch yourself. In this attitude, you probably just sneak around the room. Now think about your goals, your tasks, the challenges that are pending. How are you going to realize these, how will you overcome them and achieve them? Do you doubt you can make it? The body stays the same, don't smile, the shoulders continue to hang, and the view remains lowered. Is there any enthusiasm for your colorful future inside of you? Ready to meet your challenges? Probably not.

Now lift your head and pull your mouth like a smiley face up. How does it feel when you think of your goals? Somewhat better, right? Take a deep breath now. Do not try to let the torso bend, you will not succeed. Breathe two or three times deep through the nose and through the mouth again. Keep your smile upright. How do you stand now? Look at your foot position: Do your toes point inwards or are they rather stable, slightly turned outwards? How is your gait now, as you go through the room with conscious breathing, raised head, and a smile on your lips?

Where are your shoulders now? Now think of your goals, the joy you will have when all these goals are achieved. How does it feel now, with the head raised? Is there anything in the world that could stop you now from achieving your goals and mastering your challenges? Look into the mirror and train to pull your mouths upwards. Smile and try to get back into bad mood again. It will not help you with drawn up mouth angles

success. We can have a smile on our face as well as a serious look and thereby improve our mood. There are only muscles that we need to train.

What did you do? Almost nothing and yet, so much.

The pleasant thing about it is that you can influence your mood without mental exertion, only by changing your body position. Thus, with the help of your body, you can first leave your languid, insulted and grumbling spirit out.

You know the saying "Chin up!". My grandfather always sent me when I was just really grumpy: "Run five times around the house, then come back". See, in fact, most of the grant was wrong. What happened? The bodywork had to improve, because bending is almost impossible.

On the other hand, I had breathed better (one also says: "Breathe first deeply!"). Running is not possible without breathing deeper.

Breath

Breath is life. Without food, we can endure it for a few days, without liquid it becomes already more unpleasant. But if we do not breathe, we change the skin color and body temperature very soon. Nevertheless, we rarely pay attention to our breathing, although it is more important than anything else. Deep and calm breathing soothes and relaxes. Therefore, we find breathing as a central theme in all meditation and relaxation exercises. The brain is better oxygenated and the thoughts become clearer. This is also one of the reasons why many smokers find smoking so relaxing. When breathing in and exhaling, the breath becomes calm and regular, and the body and mind relax. Take care of your breathing and let fresh, energetic airflow through your nose deeply and breathe out all worries and fears with the air. Notice how big you are when you take your shoulders back and stretch your chest slightly. Excessively exaggerate a little, and feel your shoulders go back with every inhalation, your chest is lifted, and your belly bulges outward. When breathing out, the whole process reverses. Also, feel how comfortable it is to pull the corners of your mouth up, watch yourself in the mirror, and smile while you breathe a few times with pleasure.

I meant this before: just put the book away and try it out. It is important to get a feel for what actually happens to you and how it affects you. Try to be aware of this a few times a day, and you will see you feel much better.

Unleashing hidden energies

But there are situations in which we do not want to do anything at all. Most of all, we can then relax to come to a state as pleasant as possible, in which we need nothing more to think about. We often fall into such situations spoken about in part I from the chapter "Important is relative" and spend our time with distractions at a low level.

In order to escape this cycle, we would need an efficient slap in the face to wake up. Who could give us one these days without risking an accusation? Only ourselves.

In a book, it is always hard to write "Close your eyes, relax and follow the instructions". Let's try it with open eyes. What feelings do you have when you think back to your childhood when you were baking cookies? I don't mean that you have been yelled at by your mother because you have eaten so much dough. Think of the smells, the warm room, perhaps it's already snowing, and the electric candles shine on the Christmas tree in the garden. Let your daydream free. How does it feel, what images are rising in you? Do you see and feel the scene from back then?

You can, of course, remember other scenes of your past.

This also works in the negative sense. For example, I always feel bad when I only smell Baileys. A couple of decades ago, I drank almost a full bottle of it on a birthday party in the course of the evening. Then, at dawn, I felt so sick that it was a real horror. I needed a whole day to recover. Since then, I am making a large bow around the chocolate cups filled with said beverage. If I only smell it, the scent makes my stomach twists. Even if I see a bottle in the supermarket, I immediately think of the party and feel its consequences.

So, we have had experiences in our past, which can be brought back to mind through certain triggers from one second to another and make us experience the emotional state once again.

The scenes mentioned have arisen by chance – it wouldn't be nice if we were able to retrieve commanding states of mind in which we were so full of energy and self-confidence. Not by chance by a trigger from the outside, but just at the moment when we need it?

The prerequisite is that the experience is stored deep enough in us and the triggering pulse is clear and strong enough.

How do we save desired emotions consciously?

Everything that happens around us during a highly emotional phase is subconsciously connected and stored with these emotions.

That is, if you are deliberately striking the open palm of the other hand three or four times, five times in rapid succession with your fist, screaming "YEEES, YEES, YEEES …" every time the "YEEES, YEES, YEEES …" with the intense "winning feeling". If there is some music in the background, this music is also stored. Check out what emotions are stored inside of you with the song "We are the Champions" by listening to the song.

The key to the success of the storage is the emotional intensity with which it is performed, and the repetition rate. You have to do the "blow and cry ritual" 10 or 15 times in a short, intense sequence while you feel and feel the joy of victory at the same time. To feel the desired feeling at this moment, that is what matters.

Furthermore, the movement and the sound must be clearly different from the sounds and movements that you do otherwise. Both must be emotional and the movement intense and clear. Of course, it is important to remember which trigger – which movement and what sound – is connected to which state. With all the emotion, however, you should be careful not to break your hand, otherwise this trigger could be associated with pain, and that is not the purpose of the exercise. So soft, but intense, unique and often repeated.

Consciously retrieving emotions

The interesting thing is when we reverse the process. Imagine you are not in winners' mood and your self-confidence is on the ground. However, you could now use a good self-confidence because you have an important date soon. You can't manage to get into that mood by concentrating because your thoughts are rushing wildly through your head and you are very stressed.

Then you can use a programmed pulse to trigger the associated emotional state. You do this by hitting your fist in the palm of your hand with the same intensity as the memory process, yelling "YEEES, YEES, YEEES …". Do this and you'll see if the programming was intense enough, you'll automatically feel put into the programmed mood. If you had heard a fiery song in the background during the winners' jubilee and the movement, this would have been associated with the feeling of the winner. In other words, if you only hear this song somewhere, you will return to the winners' mood. If you drive by car, make a short stop, insert the song and knock in while you are roaring.

Train a few movement patterns, just as athletes often do. They thereby bring themselves into the desired condition, into the condition, which has enabled them many times to bring top performances at a given moment. The movements should be slightly adapted to the desired mood. You do not have to jump around in the room before the meeting or before the sex, hit the palm with your fist and yell "YEEES, YEES, YEEES …".

It also suffices subtle programming, such as the rubbing of the knuckles with the other hand or the unobtrusive pressing on a certain point on the arm. If, however, you are in front of thousands of spectators, a loud, explosive scream and clenched fist might be better. Let your creativity run wild and program the appropriate trigger for different emotional states. One for creativity - think of "Wickie and the Strong Men". Whenever a solution is required, Wickie rubs his nose and he becomes creative.

Save a trigger for pure joy, one for gratitude, a subtle for self-confidence at meetings and a tender for erotic hours. The imagination knows no limits. It is also a movement without sound, it is only important that it is a movement that is not normally found in everyday life. Cleaning your nose, hand shaking, etc. would not be particularly memorable.

Without exercise and training, many anchors are lost or simply forgotten. Strengthen these whenever you are in the appropriate feeling. For example, if you've just been very self-confident when you've won something, or when you've done a great creative job.

Pay attention to frequent repetitions and the emotions during the repetition.

Energy level

Ask yourself the question: "How good or bad is my mood right now?" and the answer is "I am stressed, annoyed and bored", please go back to the section "What are words and how do they work?" In the chapter "Your own language". Make yourself aware of what is discussed there, right now, it is important. Not you as a complete person "are", but something is generalized and placed above everything else.

Through a generalized questioning, we can get into a bad mood.

If we think about the level of energy on which we are at that moment, we have something that we can change. It is not us, but it is the level of energy that is not sufficient at the moment. Do not judge yourself, but the power level on a scale of 0-10. Zero means in a transcendent sense: I am in a miserable mood the world can now perish from me! Ten means: superior mood, everything is perfect, I love life. If you now say: "My level is at minus three", then we formulate the question again. "What level of energy would I need now to solve the problem, to cope with the stress and feel good?"

If you answer "plus 15", you will realize that some action is needed to reach that level. It is again about making oneself aware of one's own condition. Then you realize quite quickly that with a power level of 3 no peak performances are possible. You do not have to worry about the current situation, but you are looking for the low energy level. Isolate this cause and dissolve it with the appropriate means. Directly and immediately you can only influence your own energy level. Only you can decide how much you can be pulled down by other things. You also have a very good energy management by directing the energy - instead of using it for anger – direct it to further targets.

How much you are being awarded can only be reduced step by step by using more differentiated themes.

Bring yourself to a maximum level with your body, breathing and programmed movements. And then you do it like Buddha and ask:

"To whom does the gift belong if I do not accept it?"

You may also reject a "gift" every now and then. Consider anything good or bad, whether interesting or idiotic, as a gift. Gifts we subconsciously associate with something pleasurable. Try it out, change the word choice. Instead of "stressful overwork", use the word

"Gift" (even if the stomach turns around at this moment). Do you notice a difference? You prefer to accept gifts, but you can also refuse them, but the tone when you reject a gift is much more friendly, than if you reject an unloved work. If you reject a gift in a friendly manner, you may encounter understanding and gain a better mood, though you probably work the most. In an annoyed state, a more nerve-racking work to take or to strike, leads in any case to bad mood. And you have the work anyway.

Self-confidence is not congenital. We can control and train it by simple means. Even small changes in our behavior have a big impact on our lives. Ask yourself several times a day: What are I now focusing on, how do I think and how do I talk about the current topic, how is my body posture, my breathing? Imagine a speedometer and be aware of your current number of revolutions. What speed would you need at the moment to achieve the best performance, and what measures are you taking now to achieve this?

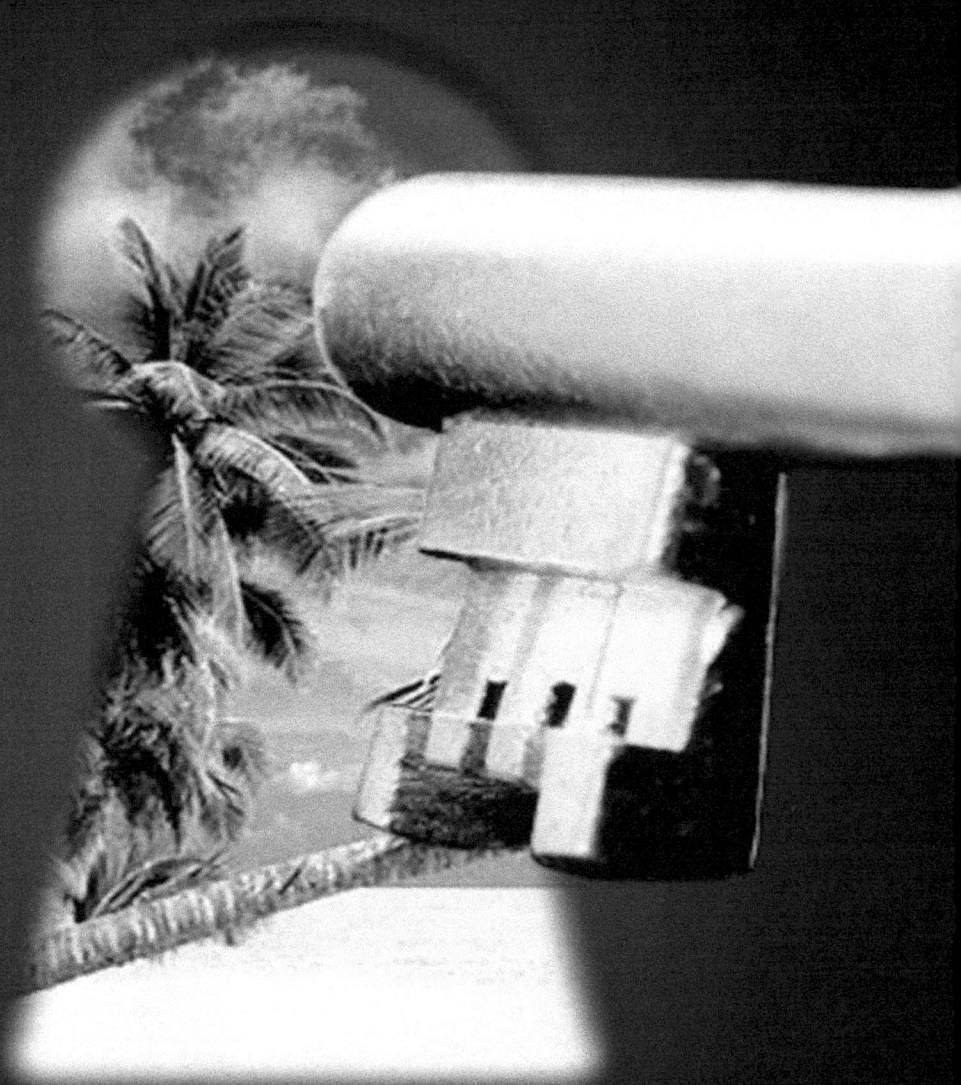

KEY 14

FREEING YOURSELF FROM WRONG BELIEFS AND CONDITIONING

Why do we believe something that is not true?

Who, like me, is Catholic, knows the sentences that are repeated in the service of God. "I am guilty, great God, by my fault, by my great fault ..." "I am not worthy that you enter under my roof..."

For me as a little boy, that was always incomprehensible, I thought God loves me, is my friend, wants to give me only good things in life. Then I hear in this important event that I am guilty of being a sinner and not worthy. All adults say this every Sunday and are very united. On the other hand, they say we are God's children; on the other hand, I am not worthy. For me, that was not understandable, because my parents would not have said that to me, I believe, even then, if I had lighted the house with all these stupid ideas I had as a kid.

But somehow you internalize the texts, perhaps also because you do not question them. Since my childhood days, I have simply left out these words, the Lord may forgive me, whether the Pope also does it, is indifferent to me.

The same applies to sayings like "Rather poor and healthy than rich and sick". I say to myself, isn't it better to say, "Rather rich and healthy than poor and sick." But each one of us has sentences in his vocabulary, which he has always heard and probably never questioned. Simply taken over by people or institutions who either pursue their own intentions with it, or by people who mean it very well, but these sentences themselves as seen and given as "correct".

The saying "Rather poor and healthy ..." is probably from the Middle Ages. It was inconvenient among noblemen to have tanned skin or to get in contact with the normal people – and especially in sexual contact. The result was a lack of sun in combination with incest. The fact that diseases under these conditions are not surprising, surely seems clear to anyone.

On the other hand, the physical activity of the rural population was strong and constant. For reasons of deficiency, these people ate almost exclusively vegetarian, and so they were spared, at least, by gout and similar illnesses.

Today, this is something different in our modern western world. Therefore, the sentence no longer applies in the traditional form. Nevertheless, it affects many of our lives, subconsciously creating a distance to wealth, because this is connected with illness.

Another, very widespread concept of belief is: "money doesn't make you happy". What is in principle right, because only the effect of money makes happy. At least at certain moments. This includes the moment when we get money. Then we have a good feeling. The other moment is when we spend it and do good things with it or do something good for others. It is not the small notes with numbers and any

Bridges on which we often spend all our time and energy – no, we're on the hunt for the moments when we feel good about the money.

We interpret the sentence "money doesn't make you happy" subconsciously, as if it was bad and useless to have a lot of money. We interpret: to be happy doesn't work if you have money. From this we conclude: Money makes unhappy. We also find plenty of examples. How extensively we are told about crises of very rich people and stars, of people we often see as role models. If it does not work for them, even though they have so much money, the correctness of the sentence is confirmed for us. We always believe in it more deeply and anchor it deeply within ourselves, as a given truth. We are not aware of the fact that not the money (but the unclear use of it) is responsible for the problems. And so, our "basement master", the subconscious, has no idea of misinterpretation and believes that money means misfortune. Since we know that we do not like bad luck, it makes sure that this can't be triggered by money at least. It keeps money away from us.

Think about which areas of your life are still affected by unreflected beliefs. What sentences do you know about money, health, happiness and wealth? Write down the sentences of your childhood and think about the effects that these sentences could have on your subconscious mind and thus on your life.

You can apply the approach described below for money in all areas.

What do you think about money?

Write down a few keywords and thoughts that come to you spontaneously when you think of money. For me it was the following:

> Freedom, independence

> Relaxation

> Luxury

> Earning money means: No time for the kids

> Stress, problems at work

> Tough work

> Frustration

> Gives me freedom but it takes a lot of energy to earn some

> Daddy is in the office from morning until evening

> I am wasting my life with senseless work

First, there were positive thoughts coming up, but then I linked money pretty quickly with work, and that became tough. Money in itself is pleasant, if one has it, but it is obviously not a comfortable thing for me to actually earn it. It is associated with renunciation, stress and anger. Subconsciously, I seem to ask myself the question: is it at all worth the effort to make a lot of money - or is it enough, to earn little money with as little effort just to get through life?

This is where a key aspect comes into play. Obviously, I have connected some extra profit with more time needed and more stress, less time with the kids, etc. This is, of course, fatal. Because of that, it is perfectly clear why I haven't gotten beyond certain basic level for a long time.

My subconsciousness is constantly working against me. Against my dream of freedom and relaxation, as long as the path leads to stressful work. Because freedom means a lot of work, a lot of trouble, a lot of stress, and of course I do not want that.

These were my own experiences – connections that most likely developed in my childhood, youth, and apprenticeship.

It becomes even worse, for not only our own impressions influence us, but (as described above) also general beliefs, which have arisen mostly long ago and under completely different circumstances.

What did you hear about money?

What beliefs about money do you know? What did your parents or grandparents say about money? How did you, in your childhood, deal with money: generous or greedy? Did it bring joy or stress?

Here are a few of my thoughts:

> Money is not everything

> Money doesn't make you happy

> Rich people can't eat more either

> I have to work hard to get money

> Only those who work hard every day can really earn a lot

> Take care of the pennies and the pounds will take care of themselves

In most people, there are many negative associations, which they have somehow recorded and subconsciously saved as true. We are constantly influencing our actions. Let's leave it standing in the room for the moment.

Now we turn the game around. Think about how your life would be better if you were financially free. Stand up, stretch and breathe deeply. Bring yourself to a top energy level, think of your trigger pulses and your breathing. And then put on good music and quickly write down everything you need to know about the freedom and joy you would have in terms of absolute financial freedom.

For me it was these points:

> Spend time with the kids much more relaxed

> Spend much more time with my wife

> Traveling around the world

> Time and money to visit the best lectures

> Weekend trips and cultural journeys to the most beautiful cities in the world

> The possibility to help others a lot

> Find time and peace to learn Spanish and other languages

> Hire a cook and therefore earn more time

> Hire the best trainers and teachers for my family and me

> Work at the most beautiful places in the world

> Never ever working for money again

> Start with new hobbies that I couldn't afford before

New doctrines

In this mood, you formulate the above mentioned negatively affected beliefs from your past so that these sentences will give you strength and energy in the future and help you achieve your goals.

Yes, for money I have to work hard and invest a lot of time. This is easy for me, because I am delighted to combine my abilities and creativity intelligently, creating products that generate bubbling sources of money that enable us to live a rich, free, relaxed and meaningful life.

Money is not everything, but with my knowledge and my feeling, I use it so that it brings me, my family and many other many beautiful experiences into life.

Write your sentences in large letters and hang them up in your daily field of view. For each negative sentence, develop a new one, or supplement it accordingly. The more emotional, the better. The new sentence has succeeded when you feel good, feel joy and motivation when reading. If you leave the new set cold or rather embarrassed, take a step back and look for the reason why your wishful thinking does not yet harmonize with your feelings. Review your goals from the beginning of the book once again in terms of consistency with your new beliefs. Are there any contradictions, or are the new beliefs exactly on target?

KEY 15

THE PERFECT ENVIRONMENT

People, moods, possibilities

Let's open up for a new kind of encounter and the possibilities will come!

Our environment, the people, their mood and the opportunities around us, are a key factor in success or failure - for perseverance or abandonment.

However, it is often very difficult for us to leave our environment, even if we have already established that it is not good for us. Whether working colleagues, friends, or your own family, we feel connected to people, spaces and countries in certain areas and would like to resolve or alter these connections and circumstances. "What could one or the other think when we suddenly break the contact or severely restrict it?".

We are thus in a network of connections, of which only a few are really beneficial. Many connections are obsolete and only ballast, others even draw energy from us. We feel committed, do not want to hurt anyone. Therefore, we prefer to keep quiet than to free ourselves from the "entanglements" of the last decades. In this state, we have little energy to build new, invigorating and effective connections.

If you have ever tried to quit smoking among smokers, then you know how hard it is. You are constantly reminded of smoking and again animated: "One is okay ...". It is much easier in a group of non-smokers. Just because nobody is constantly doing it in front of you.

In a group of successful, open-minded people, it is also easier to find support, confirmation or stimulus for new business ideas than under eternal misgivings and black painters. Even the energy is different. An energy that makes everything seem feasible is an incredibly driving and inspiring force.

In plants we can see the relevance of the right environment daily. The same plant in a small pot remains smaller than the other in the larger pot.

With the same pot size the sun hours and the water supply of the plant decide about growth or just survival.

How do we find the perfect environment?

If you are ready to embrace certain changes, it is easy to find the right environment. The environment that supports our visions and goals. Regarding sport, this is obvious. If I like to play tennis, I should register in a tennis club. The question then arises as to whether I choose my own local club or the super club in the next city. Crucial is what I am willing to invest to find a better environment. What kind of effort would I like to learn from players who are currently better than me? This is the same in business life! Proximity means opportunities! The proximity to the people who could give us orders increases the chance of getting a new order significantly! Let us take the proverb "out of eyes, out of mind" in reverse:

"In the field of view, in mind"

Take, for example, Silicon Valley, the technology center of the world. Here, basic conditions have developed which make new inventions and developments easy. Here it is normal to do something "not normal". From this environment unbelievable products are produced, which otherwise would not have fallen on fertile soil and would have reached maturity.

Just go and find the people you need. Move, even if you do not know the direction yet.

Running with a head full of ideas around a trade fair in Germany and finding partners for the development is a tedious and frustrating business. We already have, we do not need, we do not care – these are the answers that you take back home. After I had tried a lot in Germany and had hardly moved on, I dared to go to Dubai.

Go to a trade fair in Dubai or anywhere else in the world and discuss ideas with others, then you will be redirected from one to the other in the positive sense until someone finds an interest in your idea. I speak from my own experience in the field of construction project control. Suddenly, I sat with a couple of sheikhs at the table to discuss concrete projects. Ideas are considered to be full and not blocked off from the start. It tries to find ways of working together. If these are often not feasible, the conversations stimulate new ideas and bring new contacts, which in the next step – as in my case – lead to good business.

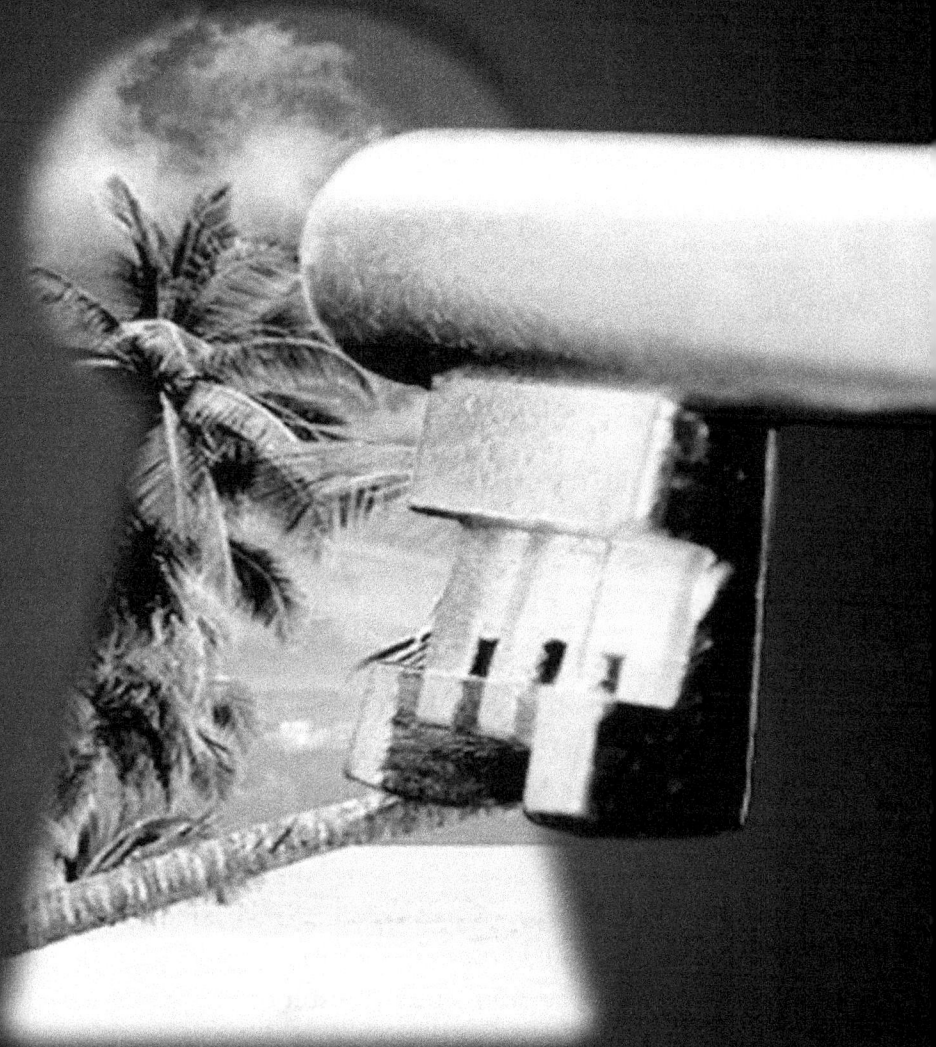
KEY 16

REDUCING DISTRACTIONS

We can be so well prepared, be physically and mentally stable, know our goals, and have perfectly prepared plans. Nevertheless, the desired success is often not achieved. A major reason for this is external influences, which distract us from our goals in different ways.

Why do we distract ourselves?

Distraction always means time loss. This can happen directly by simply killing our time with things that are not conducive to us and our goals.

On the other hand, distraction happens when we are not sure and ask others for advice. This advice is often not useful for a variety of reasons. Especially if we need basic advice. Nobody knows my goals as exactly as I do. How can someone know how to help me reach them?

I was always particularly vulnerable when I was not sure about my cause, or I almost did not care where the "journey" was. Then I asked all sorts of friends and acquaintances about their opinions and puzzled about the deeper meaning of the answers. It took me a long time to realize that it didn't help me much. Everyone had their own challenges to master and could and wanted to care about my issues only on the side. I was secretly awaiting answers to questions for my life, for my life path, yes, that my goals were right. People had their job, the most since the apprenticeship in the same company. What should be the result of this search for advice and confirmation? In discussions with nice, friendly and helpful people who had very different goals, different living conditions and other experiences …? You sense it: distraction and uncertainty. Because I appreciate these friends very much and value their opinion. In this area, however, they could not help me.

My eyes were opened after years by George S. Clason, with his classic literature "The richest man of Babylon".

In this book, he describes a hardworking worker who receives advice from the richest man. Before that he had given all his savings to a brick-burner, so that he could travel to the neighboring country to buy jewelry at a favorable price. This jewelry should be resold after the return with profit. The worker had lost everything. The brick burner was one

trustworthy man, a friend, but not a jewelry expert. The mistake was: he asked someone for help, who had no idea in this area. He had turned to him because he trusted him in other areas. I would never come up with the idea to ask my best friend how to repair my bike, if he is a baker and has no relation to motorcycles. Logically, right? No one would. We often overlook (and I can certainly call it that way) that we subordinate other abilities that they simply do not have.

With the life, the goals, the problems, it isn't that easy, good advice is hardly to be found. Who is talking about who can help us? Most people are struggling with their own challenges and have no time or nerves to listen to the worries of others, to discuss them and to work out solutions.

Then, of course, there are specialists for each area. But these are, as the name suggests, responsible only for individual areas. A full-scale "project support for life" is not possible for most of the time and content.

The only way to reduce this type of distraction and to integrate the advice of others is to make the question more precise.

Only on precise questions you can expect useful answers. In order to be able to formulate these questions, however, you need to know what you want. We can't stop by. Only if you ask qualified, you can correctly classify the answers and assess them as conducive or obstructive. For qualified questions on specific topics you will find, in addition to friends, experts who can give you answers. Decide how to deal with the advice, but do not completely change your target direction, but only fine-tune it.

The clearer you know your goals, the more accurately you can formulate the questions and the more specific the answers. These will help you to continue your way as before, or make easy course corrections. Both are very time-efficient and goal-oriented. If you do not know your goals exactly, you are constantly thrown out of the way by too much advice, which costs time, money and nerves and is not purposeful.

Self-interest of others

Sometimes those who are asked for advice do not want to give a qualified and honest opinion due to envy or personal interest.

After an eight-hour flight across the southern Pacific we arrived in the middle of the night in Tahiti. I wanted to make it comfortable in a dark corner at the airport, when two young ladies, about my age, asked me if they could stay here. Of course, I didn't mind. We fell asleep soon.

After a short time, a man woke us up, whom I should later baptize the "rogue". He invited us to his backpacker's villa and promised the transport there and the others

Night hours were free. Why not, I thought, and we went. Everything was perfect, but when he wanted my passport in the morning, the mood changed. Especially because he now announced that the first night was only free when the second was also spent with him.

I was so annoyed that I did not get any information in the backpacker's villa, but went straight by bus to the harbor. I found the "Aurora Nui", two weeks she was a supply ship, for 60 dollars I could go with.

Two weeks pure South Sea, including black pearls and incredibly friendly people. No tourist but me. It was like in another time. We usually stayed anchored overnight, near a village. There was enough time for bathing, wandering around and living with the locals. This trip was one of my most intense and beautiful travel experiences ever.

Back to Tahiti, I immediately took the opportunity to book another boat trip. However, the ship did not leave until two days later. So, I got back in contact again with the "rogue". The place was perfect, right on the black sand beach, and the "rogue" had already forgotten me. My "old acquaintances" looked at me from the airport with big eyes. Stunned, they listened to my reports. "But the Tuamotus are closed to tourists, because of drinking water shortages and mosquito bursts," they said. I heard about this for the first time. Water scarcity was by no means the case, for it often rained at night and the water barrels were full. There was also no mention of a mosquito plague.

The "rogue" had assured its guests that there was no way to travel there. The laziness and also the inexperience of the ladies (and some other guests), made them believe it. The result was: they traveled around the world and did not make it back from the backpacker to the dreamlike islands of the South Seas.

The personal interest of the club owner was to keep as many guests as possible for as long as possible. He succeeded.

This example can be applied to many areas of life. We are making great efforts ... and then, just before it really becomes interesting, let ourselves be distracted from our goal.

Perhaps I too would have braced myself of the supposed dangers if I had to take responsibility for another person. For example, for my children or for my girlfriend. This is why it is also important to ask precisely: what would someone like to achieve, who gives me information? I should do that before I adjust my goals to it.

In everyday life, this kind of distraction often takes place through advertising. Fears of the future are fueled and then the protection of children and the family is propagated. Accident, storm, hail, property and life insurance companies surpassed the need for help and protection. Of course, not everything is unauthorized. It becomes critical when we are too intimidated by fear-making and therefore change our way.

In the profession, fear is also used as a means of power, so that it is possible to work as long as possible, hard and against low wages. Fear, that another could make it better and cheaper and I could lose my job. With this fear, you can easily control yourself and not really notice how your own life passes by. It does not happen to you, if you know nothing else. The animation program from the "rogue" was certainly interesting. It only faded when it was compared to two weeks of South-South cruise.

I have adopted my motto for such cases by Bruce Springsteen:

„When they said: 'sit down' I stood up!!"

Envy

The distraction through envy I experienced when I began with coaching and lectures. I was new to this area, trying to build a network - committed people who support each other and work together. There were numerous conversations and appointments, I worked out concepts and discussed for a long time. It did not matter (at least not to me). Because, in the final analysis, everyone is self-sufficient and has enough to do with his own themes. In particular, the initial phase of new projects with supposed partners or network partners is to start from my experience only when I know my product, absolutely convinced of it and let the benefits for the customer shine with enthusiasm. If that is the case, I can take partners for certain areas. But not before that, because otherwise we get a lot of distractions and uncertainties. And if success occurs on one side, the envy won't take long to show up. It often leads to the end of the relationship.

In my company for construction project management, we had our core area, and then we were able to bring other companies into the boat in order to optimize the product for the client. The threads, however, were kept in our hands.

So, it came that we provided many companies with orders, but through some contacts also good orders for us emerged.

> *Distractions - whether caused by the outside or by ourselves - must be recognized, judged in their value, and repelled in the correct measure, or even taken as an occasion for slight course corrections.*

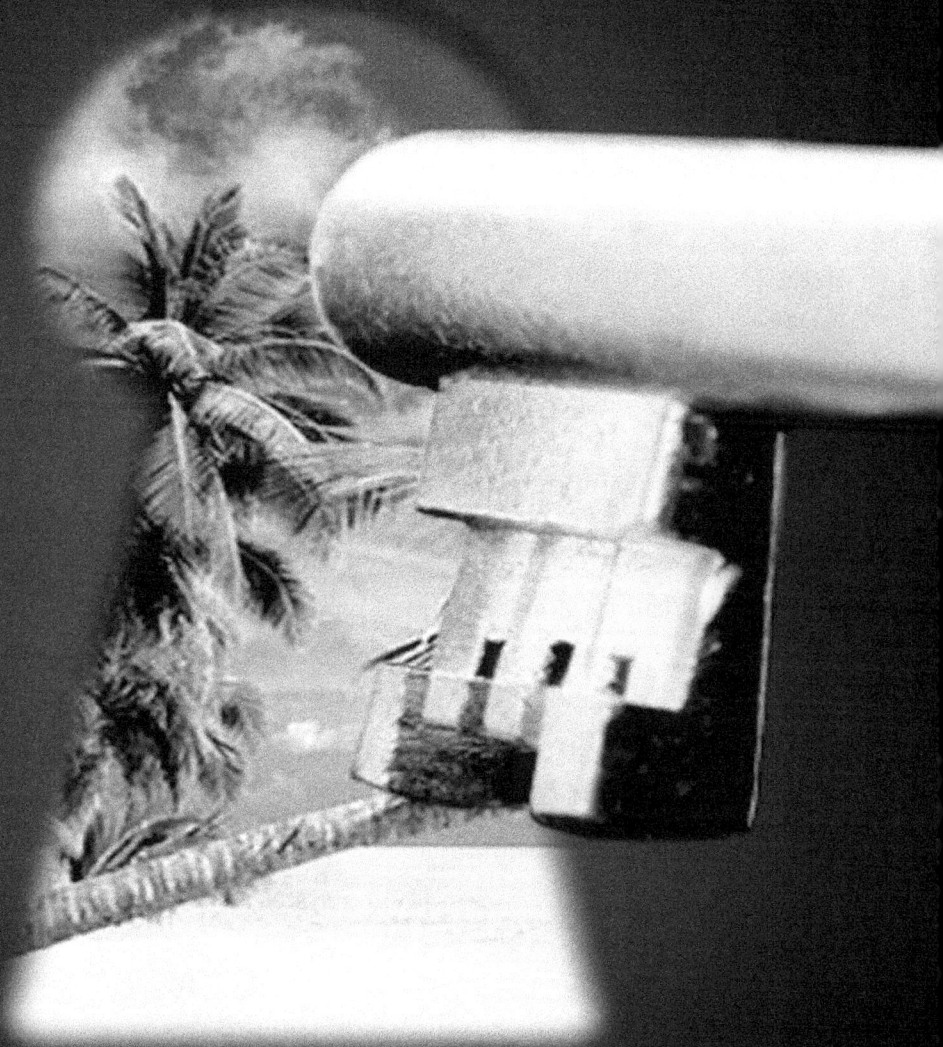

KEY 17

FILTERING THE OVERFLOW OF INFORMATION

The way to more time is to recognize and remove the superfluous.

For the evaluation of food, we have developed filter systems over the course of thousands of years. No one eats food that already smells weird. We smell "the roast" and act according to it. We spit out sour milk, we recognize moldy vegetables and throw it away. At least three filter systems protect us from spoiled food. Other systems on our tongue tell us when we are full of food and prepare the digestive processes. The human being has switched off this measuring system for the saturation level by means of additives in many foodstuffs, so it can be refilled unstopped and the excess calories can be converted nicely into fat. If the natural filters are deliberately bypassed during the diet – what do you think, how often will consideration be given to unprotected systems?

Even though you can often see all the hairs standing up while listening to the radio because of the witless babble, the idea of having to listen to ten channels at the same time is even worse.

In technology, there are very simple filter systems, with the help of which the frequency at which the favorite transmitter is transmitted can be selected. All other frequencies remain silent and do not interfere.

Unfortunately, people find the filtering in daily life somewhat more difficult. Without a break, more and more things are pounding on us. The possibilities of communication allow, yes, they demand, the constant accessibility and the active participation in this "game", which we could also call madness. This morning, an acquaintance told me that his 16-year-old nephew was so compelled to answer all the messages on his smartphone that he had little time to shower. After 20 minutes in the bathroom, he was so much behind with the answer that he almost couldn't catch up ...Time for productive and thus satisfying work remains almost no longer there.

How is it possible to protect ourselves and our family against such negative influences?

Active and passive filtering systems

Active filter systems must recognize what they have to filter, they must be aware of what is disturbing, and then they must actively seek and act.

For passive systems, the sieve is a good example: it simply leaves everything that is smaller than its mesh width.

It is useful, as is so often the case in life, to install a combination of both systems: a passive basic filter and a targeted active filter.

We have talked about the great impacts of these words on us. The own, the words of acquaintances, friends and strangers. Words and texts from the television, the radio, the press, the Internet. They are coming from all sides. Most of the news and information is negative, sad, frightening. It is no wonder that with the constant consumption of this information we are also in a negative, aggressive mood. Even if we are actively looking for recreational entertainment, we rarely find a film – whether for adults or for children – that does not include aggression, intrigue, murder and other violence.

We can install passive filters and simply do not provide a TV, a radio or an Internet. The problem is: to not allow anything at all is exactly the opposite. The hunger for the forbidden is, as is known, the strongest, and each one of us develops his greatest abilities in this area, in order to get the desired. It is no longer possible to swim with the trend a bit. The pressure to be there is growing ever more in the kindergarten, in school, in studying, in work and in leisure time.

"WHAT, you do not know, you did not look at it?" We are not there anymore, if we do not reply immediately, we are not informed, because we are not talking together for a long time. Involuntarily, every human being is brought into a situation which perhaps does not suit him, but he does not come out. He often only has the choice to participate or be marginalized.

Nevertheless, it is useful to set certain rules for themselves and for their children. Rules that specify what, how long and why can be consumed. When the smartphone pauses and the Internet line is out of order. Surprisingly, many survive this

"Drug depletion" quite well, if the reasons are solid.

The only way to protect yourself is to have a good reason, which is more important than the participation in this media theater. Here I speak of active filters. While it is not that easy to find these reasons and believe in them, we are fortunate to have many topics to help us. When I ask my son the question of whether he believes that Cristiano Ronaldo can play football so much because he has been watching TV all the time, or whether he has learned it because he has been doing ambitious exercises every day. This acts like an electric shock and immediately tears him away from the TV.

I know it's a simple example, but there's a lot to it.

Why does it seem like that? Because the boy sees a goal that is more important to him than anything else. He focused and he dreamed of the World Cup. While playing football, the world can go down beside him. Active filter systems are targets and their values against the deflections. Unfortunately, however, distractions are much more promoted than clear goals and the teaching of how to achieve them. Our task as parents or superiors is to recognize the goals of the people around us. Then we have to help them create the space they need to achieve their goals. We need to provide them with tools and backup so that they can defend themselves against distractions, exclusion and resistance, and go step by step. In it, I see the task for each of us. We must begin with ourselves.

Why does it not work without filtering systems anymore?

Most of us have no filter systems at all. They have never had any and still have somehow gotten through. The time has been less aggressive in terms of information flow and access. Times have changed drastically. When we turned the dial of the gray or green telephone 30 years ago for a tele-control and watched as the disk of 9 rattled back, we could still make it cozy next door. Today, three messages are to be received and written. There's no time left, that's stress. Without a filter system, this becomes too much. We let everything go on around the clock, without thinking about what it costs us every day.

> By which of your employees does the radio run in the background all the time?

> Who will react immediately to every message, in whatever form and at what time it arrives in your smartphone?

> How often does a message throw you out of focus on what you are doing?

> How often do you answer a call, even though you are in a private conversation with someone?

> How much time do you lose daily? How much energy do you lose? How much work do they have?

> In addition, with this behavior, you also run the risk of being surprised and unprepared. You do not know what message you are expecting in the next moment. Although you can't filter the contents of the incoming messages, you can actively set the time when you receive them. Thus, you can prepare your physical and mental condition so that you will find a solution, whatever it may be, in peace.

Priority of the distraction

In twelve years of project management and construction management, I initially received calls, e-mails and SMS, which were to be evaluated as follows:

Category 1:

Mr. Schwarz, my hammer has dropped, shall I pick it up again? Or similar serious cases.

Frequency approx. 70%, time expenditure by interruption, deflection of the called.

Category 2:

Those that are so important that if I do not react immediately, the world stops turning. I come to the construction site and the problem has already been solved in 90% of the cases, or it needs a little thought effort to solve it.

Frequency about 29%, great time expenditure due to interruption, distraction, uncertainty of all involved.

Category 3:

Something really happened, the gas line was damaged, the fire brigade evacuated the neighbors building, it would be good if you could come quickly.

Frequency approx. 1%, time expenditure in the individual case indeed high, but extremely rare.

The categories can be transferred almost to any environment. Why do most people accept to be bothered by every little thing?

Through the many communications and the constant employment connected with it, the impression is of great importance among others. In our business, it is still true: who does a lot is important, who does not have much to do, must at least pretend as if. Those who prefer to continue to make a career, and those with whom they usually do to have. Who is busy is important and who is important is indispensable and deserves more. These people often deserve more, but the question is: at what price? What actually lies behind this behavior and the unbelievable urge to apply, later on in the chapter "Behavior patterns from childhood".

We should quickly learn to channel these interruptions and constant accessibility so that there is enough space and energy for us and our goals. Refer to fixed times, where you are available for questions, not rude, but definitely. These are also active filters, which give you time for concentrated work.

Negative messages

Negative information takes energy from us. Energy, which we urgently need for innovations, for ideas and their implementation.

Our ears, for example, are always active, they take care of everything, round the clock. Fortunately, we have systems like "selective listening". Our brain checks all incoming information and sounds and decides whether they are important or unimportant to us. The important is followed by a corresponding reaction; the unimportant remains unaffected. When sleeping, it reveals to us the slightest, unknown noise as a danger and makes us watchful. Familiar and partly much louder noises do not get us out of our sleep.

Selective hearing also works naturally when we are awake. Whether we perceive noises consciously or unconsciously, our brain is activated and we consume energy. This happens with good and bad noises as well as with good or bad news. The difference is just: bad news also hit us on the Mood, also subconscious. Certain words such as "war", "murder", "fraud", "famine" "Tax increase" etc., which run in the background on the radio, weigh our mood, even though we do not realize it. They take our euphoria and enthusiasm, they show us boundaries, dangers and disadvantages everywhere.

The eyes see images of suffering and horror every day, Europe has now become a fortress, and we feel threatened by the refugees from the south and the east. Fear of wars, refugees, fear of the workplace, the children. Murder and manslaughter, fraud and bribery. Ever lower interest rates on savings, uncertainty about the pension and rising taxes and cost of living also create fear of the future. The two-society society is cemented with vigor and power. This situation worries us all, no matter how much money we have in the account. These negative scenarios are presented to us daily in various forms. No wonder, then, that hearing and seeing often goes by. The increase in tinnitus and visual disturbances could be an indication that many things do not go well here.

Do you want to do this, to constantly consume negative news and information, just to be "informed" and "to have a say"? Do you have a common understanding based on information that is often very subjective and that you can hardly react to, except by worrying more?

Positive messages

Fear is important as long as it does not paralyze us and we do not sit like the rabbit in front of the snake. Let's avoid the snake as far as possible. There are also good news, but they can't be sold that well, so they are in the background

Let's see the good news, for example: we have no war in Germany, we have an information system with the Internet, which enables us to reach the whole world in seconds. Manipulation and fraud can be kept much more secret than before. Children at least have more rights and opportunities in Europe than ever before. Animal welfare and environmental protection are public issues, although still weak, but still. We have the opportunity to visit doctors and we do not have to be hungry.

I have decided to see almost no more news, almost not watching TV at all, and reading newspaper only once a week. A few information channels on the Internet, of which I feel well-informed, and that's it.

It was too energy-intensive and time-consuming to feed me daily, indeed hourly, with information that does not bring me anything for which I can do nothing and which I can't change at the moment.

This is a step towards the sentence:

> *"Lord, let me change what I can change, let me accept what I can't change, and let me always be better at distinguishing one from the other."* Reinhold Niebuhr

What I hear and see, I can largely change. However, it is a great challenge to swim against the current. It is also not always successful, and many give up and turn around. However, I can tell from my own experience that the moment you have so deeply ingrained the reasons for your reduced consumption in relation to information, and you believe in yourself, your goals and your way, you will go through it. Do not mind how others deal with their time, pay attention to your time, protect them, and decide how valuable it is to you.

Your time is worth more than gold, and the older you get, the more the value increases. So now invest in your time and use it for your goals. It is the best facility you can choose, and it is a wonderful feeling to have done it.

this over the years. In mathematics, I've never been a genius, but that doesn't bother me either.

Decades later I sit with my wife in our own kitchen at the dining table, outside it is already dark, and she tries to explain to me some legal matters. I'm already tired, the kitchen clock ticks. I do not understand much about what she wants to explain to me. But I notice how I get more annoying and react very aggressively after a short time. This situation is repeated over and over again, on different topics, including those I understand. Nevertheless, many "discussions" end among these framework conditions in the dispute. The smallest supposed impulse, which suggests to me that I am not good enough, immediately triggers aggression from the finest. If we are in other premises or outdoors, then that is

Threshold for anger and dispute much higher than when we talk in the evening, in the kitchen, while the clock is ticking.

I was not aware of the context for a long time, and I only came up with it when I began to discuss the subject of my own patterns.

The optimal conditions for my behaviour are the kitchen, a ticking kitchen clock and the evening lighting. The trigger is a thought, a word that I interpret for myself as "I am not good enough," which puts me in a state of anger and aggression that I have linked with these framework conditions in my childhood. This is the supposedly negative side of our childhood patterns.

How do we recognize disturbing patterns?

Look at yourself. How would you describe yourself? Write down three of your typical reactions that interfere with them. There should be reactions occurring several times a week. Based on the response, we will try to figure out the underlying patterns that are stored scenarios.

How do you react? Will you be aggressive, get scared or flee, and say nothing more? Under what circumstances do you become sad, irritated or frustrated?

Write down what has happened in the last two minutes before the reaction begins, describe the framework as exactly as possible. Where are you, is it evening or morning, did you just come back from work, are you watching TV, are the children screaming, or do you have to do something unpleasant? What has been said or not spoken out at all? For example, come home in good spirits, lock the door and yell "hello" through the house. No one answers, although everyone must have heard. What is the feeling that is rising in you, what reaction does it solve? Write down the framework conditions for each of the three responses.

I am sure you will come across many situations where very similar circumstances have been the trigger for your reaction. If this is the case, this is already a decisive step towards the solution. You have become aware of what you put into this mood and can be careful to avoid these conditions in the future. This does not mean you should not come home after work. But perhaps you can forgo the blanket exclamation "Hello!", And go to each one individually and greet her or him with a warm embrace. For example, I avoid evening meetings in the kitchen when a clock ticks in the background.

How can we change and dissolve patterns?

The avoidance of circumstances and situations is, of course, not always possible, especially if other persons are involved. We can hardly forbid them to use certain words, because they trigger something that does not contribute to a good mood. I would like to describe a method I learned from Anthony Robbins, an American personality trainer. I can not say where this one comes from, but I can say about some of my patterns: it works.

Once you have detected the scene, you can resize it. Change the images in your imagination, bring in different tones, colors and shapes. Change the viewing speed and film direction. What do you mean with that? Override the stored operations. This is done with the "Delete Cookies" command in the Web browser.

Put yourself in the scene, which is the basis of the unwanted reaction. Visualize the environment and listen to the words spoken at the time.

Now you start to change the whole thing, the crazier, the better. Show off funny music, see everything in light blue, the words are spoken with comic voices, people wear Viking clothes and green beards so long that they reach to the ground. The whole scene is commented on by cackling chickens. Let the film run forward and backward in front of your mind's eye, slowly and quickly, and faster and faster. In the craziest colors, shapes and noises. Do it so long until you have to smile about it. Destroy the stored data packet of this scene, which has repeatedly forced you to an unintended reaction by making it seem ridiculous. The more emotional you get, the more you involve body, mind and soul, and the better the scene is dissolved.

Repeat the process ten or fifteen times fast. You can check if the data is overwritten by thinking of the scene from then. If the pictures of your head cinema come to your mind and draw a smile on your lips, the action was successful.

In the short term, you can practice the visualization with a method that a friend of mine uses in meetings. One of the reviewers had brought her and her colleague very often to the white heat by his aggressive and pointed-type manner. There were often very emotional and unproductive meetings. The ladies used drastic means and manipulated their own point of view. Whenever the colleague spoke, they imagined a condom on his nose. My acquaintances told me, with tears of joy, how amusing the discussions had become for them and their friend suddenly. They were no longer in a position to give the colleague strict looks, but could only look him in the face with a mischievous smile. This led, as I was told, to him to immediately reduce the aggressiveness, and the discussions were factual and productive.

This was just a brief tear to show how distractions are slumbering inside us and can also surprise us completely into unwanted moods. It makes clear how we react to external circumstances and signals without wanting it, and how incredibly long-term and intensively we can be influenced by it.

Pay particular attention to the fact that you frequently fall into the same state, although there is no serious reason for this.

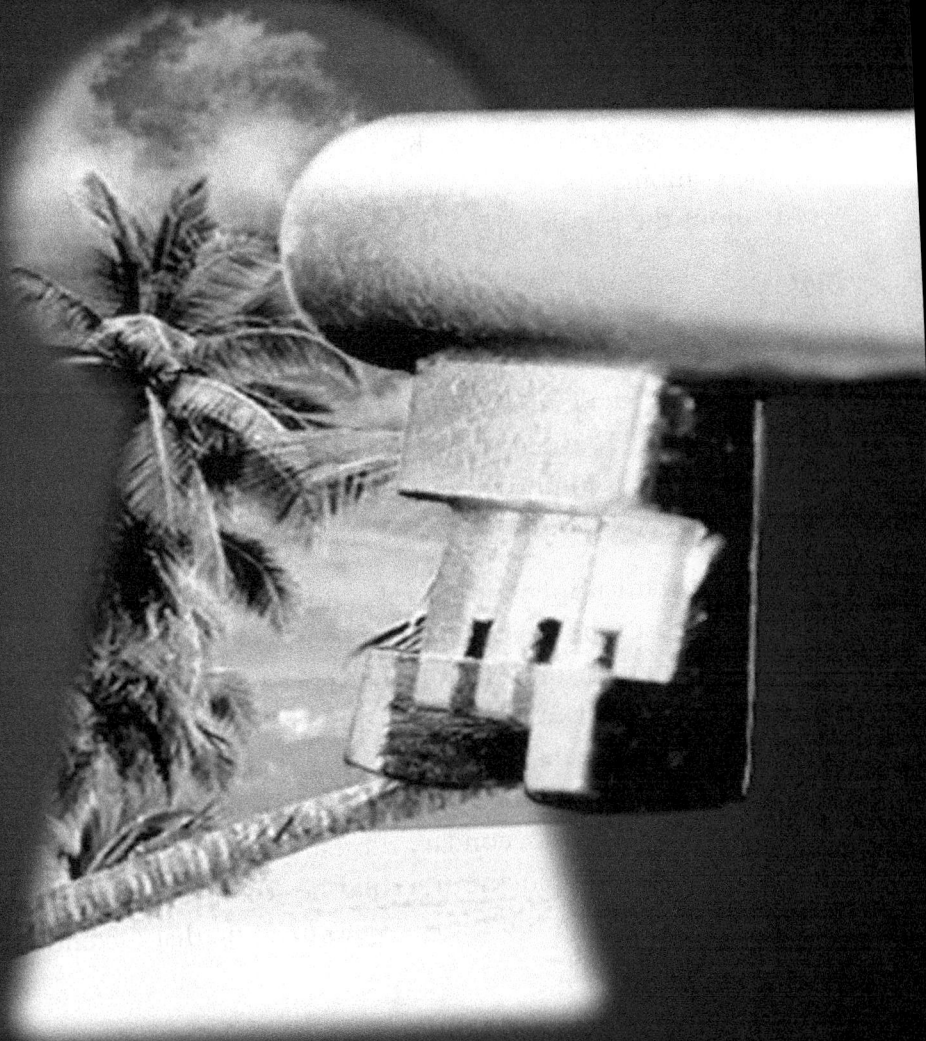

KEY 19

SECURE YOUR ENERGY SUPPLY

"In the long run, only power helps", is a commercial slogan. Without drive power, everything uses us nothing, but without the previous measures the power does not bring us much, because it is ineffective. As is so often the case, the combination of the parts that make the success. Therefore, a few words about the power supply.

Diet

The foods that we eat are called life resources because they are resources for life. Unfortunately, most of the edible products have no longer earned the name "food". To discuss and carry out the reasons for this would not help us. For us, it is important to focus on the solution, and this can only lie in our own consciousness and appropriate action.

Diabetes, myocardial infarction, stroke, hypertension, cancer, or nervous disorders ... Those who are not affected by themselves are at least someone who suffers from these or similar illnesses. The number of cases is dramatic. One cause of most diseases is the quality and composition of the "fuel" that humans use. Humans are resilient, vital, powerful and life-threatening when their supply of nutrients is guaranteed. Protein, fats, carbohydrates, vitamins, minerals, herbal secondary substances and trace elements - these substances are building blocks for a solid health. If one of these building blocks is permanently missing, it is easy to imagine that the entire system suffers or collapses under load.

Imagine a house where the heating is missing. In summer, at pleasant temperatures, this is no problem. It is uncomfortable in winter, without heat source the house is not habitable. In addition, the water pipes freeze and go broken. Water emerges from the pipes and moistens the masonry. During the next frost, the plaster bursts off in damp areas, thus the protective layer for the masonry is absent in the summer. The walls are getting wetter, mold is forming ... All because of one "Block". In the body, this is similar, we simply do not notice it immediately, if we are missing a building block among many. We only notice it when symptoms such as fatigue and / or susceptibility to injury occur. The imbalance of the diet, the lack of vital ingredients and a bad balance between active times and recreational phases usually mean a tightrope walk between "just standing" and a burn-out syndrome.

In our food, there are hardly any ingredients in sufficient quantity that we need to maintain and restore our health. The demand can only be covered by high-quality food which is as natural as possible. Especially in stress situations or during regeneration phases after a disease our body has an increased demand for all nutrients. But how gently are we treating ourselves in is regeneration phase? We have to catch up on what's left behind and often give even more gas than usual.

As already mentioned, we can only improve what we can measure. In the blood our health is reflected. To find out whether a module is missing or if one "Weakens", we need a meaningful blood count. Blood has many tasks in the body. It transports oxygen and nutrients to the organs, it ensures the return transport of degradation products of the metabolism and supports the defense against toxins and pathogens. In the case of injuries, for example, blood platelets rapidly stop bleeding. Let the most important building blocks such as magnesium, omega-3 fatty acids, vitamin D, selenium, iron, cholesterol and protein be checked at least once a year. The same applies to your PH value. Go for a specialist of your trust.

How do you deal with your own health? The following should also apply:

"Better safe than sorry!"

Break

Running continuously under full throttle is not useful for anyone in the long term. On the one hand, in the event of permanent overstressing, the performance decreases, on the other hand the health risks increase. The term burn-out is on everyone's lips, the downtime increases, the average duration of illness increases, the damage for humans and enterprises is getting bigger.

A main reason for this is not short-term peak performance, but it is the permanent overload in several areas at the same time. Professional pressure and overtime, school problems of the children, financial bottlenecks despite full employment, uncertainty about their own future, and not least doubt about whether our lives are going in the right direction. You are sure to know a lot of other things that you are burdening. Perhaps it is the parents who need care, or the relationship that is massively affected by stress.

How do we manage to get some air? Studies have shown that short but regular breaks greatly improve the performance and effectiveness of the work. Try it, it's simple and instantly effective. No matter what you are doing, you will have a time-out after fifty minutes after completing each task for five minutes. This does not mean discussing with your colleagues or checking the private e-mails quickly. There are five minutes in which you can calmly close your eyes and concentrate only on your breathing. If it is possible, lay flat and allow the pressure to flow away. Even with complex challenges and planning, you will not be thrown out of the concept. It is often the case that you use this method to come up with new, good ideas without being consciously looking for them.

It is unusual in our society to be only for oneself, and that regularly. We usually feel that nothing is going to happen during this time, but this time is incredibly valuable and improves the quality of our daily work. It does not mean that all your problems are solved, but you take the foot consciously of the gas several times a day and help your body and mind to breathe and regenerate. Train yourself to really do that every day more. Your time, by the way, will not be scarce, but on the contrary, you will see: through the breaks your productivity increases. Privately, you can use the added time and energy immediately for pleasant things. In this way, you will come step by step to a good, relaxed, and therefore very productive, state that does not touch you. Check again your schedule for the next project, if you have really planned the break times as fixed components.

Exhaustion

*Exhaustion often comes from the lack of sense
of employment.*

The meaning we assign to our task is crucial to how powerful we are. If we do not make any sense in a thing, it is difficult for us to get out of our hands. We are the only ones who can give meaning to our tasks.

If it makes sense for you to create an outstanding presentation with which you can inspire, the hours will pass like in flight. They work and work down to the last detail and enjoy it. No trace of fatigue. However, if you want to work out an endless list whose tasks are senseless from your point of view, you will be able to look at the clock in the minute clock and hardly be able to keep your eyes out of fatigue.

Make sense of your tasks! Find reasons why this task is important. In the final analysis, this means nothing but the anticipation of the desired final state and its amenities. Tasks have a meaning if they lead to an improvement in the situation. Review the previous chapters to see how these tasks fit into your goals and how they can help you achieve your goals.

Certainly, much work is not exactly on the way to your goal, which also makes nothing, as long as it is only small deviations and not complete course change. Dissatisfaction and tiredness are the result when we have the feeling that we are constantly struggling to make work that is not effective for us. These are also signs of thinking about how to change the situation. Perhaps it is time to talk to the boss and discuss another task. Only who says what he wants has the chance to get it. Just read the chapter on "What is our self-awareness?" Before you go to the boss.

Water – Elixir of life

"Where water is, there is life", that many years ago a Tunisian Bedouin told me. I was fourteen years old and on my first African safari, at that time still with my parents. The words have burnt into my head, and only in the course of time has I become more and more aware of the importance of water. Because we have a lot of good water here in Bavaria, we often do not think that it could be scarce elsewhere. We have little reference to the liquid, which rushes clear and cool from the line. But it is it that allows us wealth and prosperity. All important cities have been built on rivers, on the lifelines of the earth, as Viktor Schauberger calls them. The high culture of Egypt developed thanks to the lifeline Nile.

Unfortunately, the water is viewed by us no longer as the life-giving miracle that it actually is. Masuru Emoto has demonstrated with water crystal photographs that water can be influenced by music and thoughts in its structure. In his books, he shows harmonious crystal forms, which were, for example, sonicated with Mozart compositions, or clumped structures from drinking water reservoirs that are exposed to environmental pollution. The effect of the water quality on the human organism can already be imagined with the help of the pictures.

For a long time Emoto, as well as Viktor Schauberger, was laughed at for his work. Meanwhile, however, science is researching explanations for these phenomena and Emoto is invited as a guest speaker to many scientific events. It is worthwhile for everyone to deal with the topic of water, because water is more than H_2O. The human being now consists of 70% water and thus it is easy to understand that the quality of our drinking and cooking water has a great influence on our body. Try to drink a lot of good water, if possible not from plastic bottles.

To explain what is meant by good water would go beyond the scope of this book, but if you are ready to allow some other thoughts (and you are, or you would not have read this book to this point) the above-mentioned authors can be looked at more closely.

It is also worthwhile to think about the "power of water". Water is already the reason for wars and conflicts – and it will be even more frequent in the future. The existence of life on earth and thus our life is dependent on water. Here we can still take influence in our sense and in the sense of our children and all generations to come. Googling, for example, the term "privatization of water supply" – you will be amazed.

Electrosmog

"In order to prevent possible health risks, BfS recommends minimizing personal radiation exposure through its own initiative." (BfS: Federal Office for Radiation Protection)

But how? What is electrosmog? The word smog is a combination of the English words smoke and fog. This is an electric smoke mist. A mixture of electrical, magnetic and electromagnetic fields. Or radiation, of which – in the eyes of the mobile network operators, insolutely – is claimed to have negative effects on the human organism.

Electrosmog is a secondary phenomenon of globalization, just as radioactive radiation has been and still is in nuclear energy generation. Both look, smell, taste and do not feel. Our normal reaction to this is: what I can't grasp with my senses, there is not or it does me nothing.

Many people have not thought about this yet. Similar to water, there are only a few thought-provoking.

To my understanding of electrosmog, the performance of electrosmog-generating devices is many times higher than that of the bioelectrical functions of human cells. The frequency of the mobile radio however is very similar to that of the cell vibration in our body and is in the gigahertz range. This means several billion oscillations per second. I can easily imagine that systems with similar frequencies are mutually influencing each other. For comparison: the power from the socket has 50 hertz, which means 50 oscillations per second. Add to this the difference in performance. A human cell works with a power of about 0.001 watts, while the transmission power of smartphones can be around 1–2 watts. This is a thousand times the power, at the same frequency, directly at the head. Who now on whom influence takes, also seems clear to me. In this context I imagine what would happen if a normal incandescent lamp was connected directly to a medium voltage overland line with several thousand volts. Surely there would be nothing left of the light bulb. In addition, the organism is aggravated by the fact that the data packets can interfere with us in very choppy impulses and thus can exert abrupt stresses on the cell.

I can imagine that these loads have a very negative effect on the cells and therefore on us.

Unfortunately, we can't quite escape it, because there are also the appropriate transmitters, which with great power and network coverage everywhere their signals to us firing. Often even through network cover several times from different directions. In buses, trains and airplanes we are best irradiated. The only thing we can do with this is at least with a headset to telephone, the mobile phone not with to take to bed or at night not directly next to the head to position. The performance decreases in the square of the distance, so we would have at least a little care in the night. If it is possible – and it is feasible, because most W-LAN systems have a power switch – then turn off this function at night. The phone should still work. In the car, it would be good if you were talking to the outside antenna.

Unfortunately, unfortunately, because of the supposed advantages of communication, it is difficult to find a hearing for these topics. It is only my heart to draw your attention to the fact that there is something we do not know yet.

In conclusion, I ask the questions as to how long asbestos was considered harmless, and when X-ray examinations in pregnant women were recognized as dangerous for mother and child.

Noise

Noise causes stress. Frequently, protection in production halls (through the German Occupational Safety and Health Code) is better protected than in private life. Unconsciously, we are able to tolerate traffic noise, fan noise from computers and air conditioning systems, noise and, of course, the almost permanent sound of the media in the background. Again, because of the abilities of our brain and the ability to selectively hear, we no longer perceive many things. Nevertheless, they are burdening our system by continually requesting "processor performance", as we have already noted. Our brain is constantly concerned with finding out what is important and what is unimportant for us. If you have the opportunity to escape from the city and go to the country, and then be lucky enough not to hear any street noise, airplanes, etc., then watch the pressure of you fall. How relaxing this works when you

To hear "nothing". You will notice that very soon you will hear a lot, that is, what you will no longer perceive. Bird twitching, the rustling of the leaves or your own breath. The pressure bell, which in the normal case overdrives everything, is also an energy consumer, which you should at least temporarily slow down, as far as that is possible.

Summary

We have gone a long way to this point. From visions to goals to their justifications, we have taken the first steps toward the goal and all areas planned cleanly. We know how to optimize our time management, can increase our self-esteem as needed and protect us from distractions. We are physically fit and healthy. Nothing stands in the way of success in our lives. Nevertheless, there are still a few points that I would not want to keep from you.

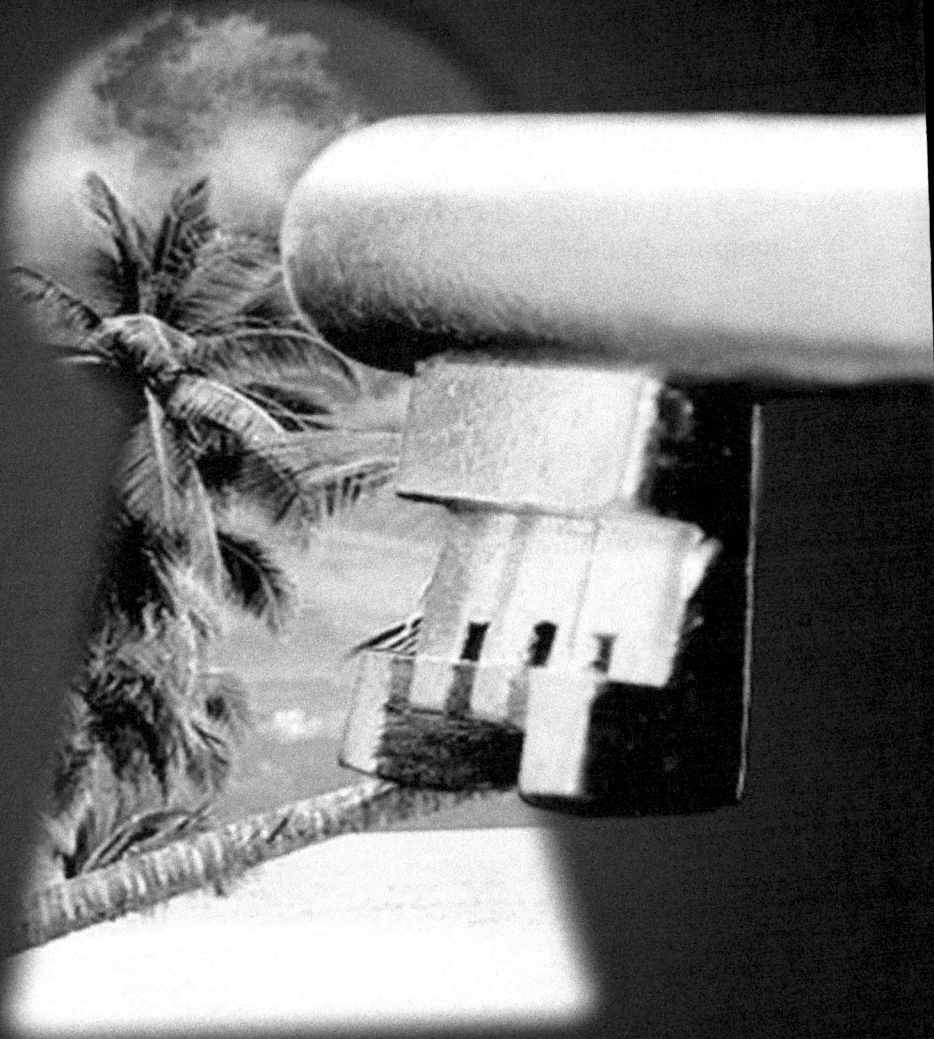

KEY 20

BEING SUCCESSFUL IS A PROCESS

When are you successful?

〉 We all need success, whether big or small. Everyone has their own views of success and failure. The only question is: who has devised these definitions? How do you know when you are successful? How did you define your success? What are your criteria for successfully completing a thing?

Are you successful if you have coped with a very large professional challenge, but have been working through it for days, created stress with your family, and have received stomach ulcers?

Are you successful if you work every day from 8:00 am to 5:00 pm and have lunch time for your children, but do not earn enough to go on holiday twice a year?

I can only improve and optimize what I can measure. But to measure something, you need guideline values and reference points.

While using the example of driving, it is immediately clear what is meant. Keep the steering wheel stiff on a straight road, or your arms are constantly moving, even if they are only very small movements. These movements are constant corrections of the direction. Your eyes are always in motion, watching the course of the road and reporting to your brain, which in turn informs your arms and hands, in what direction and how far you should turn the steering wheel. At the same time, you control the vehicle speed with regard to the maximum permissible speed, pay attention and react to road signs, adjust your driving conditions to the road conditions. In addition, you perceive and react to the dangers and distractions of other road users. By the way, you will not let your goal go.

You'll notice, driving is a constant process of measuring, correcting, re-measuring and correcting. Your eyes and ears are the measuring sensors and your arms and legs are the executive organs. The brain is used to coordinate and evaluate the measures. You have clear guidelines as to whether you are successful or not by the road, the traffic regulations and the road signs. You are successful if you reach your goal without a taut, accident-free, relaxed and punctual.

What are your benchmarks for success?

Write down three defining features in the private sphere, under which you would describe yourself as successful and feel so. Then do this also for the professional field.

> ❯   I am successful in my private life when:

> ❯   Consider where the origin of these success definitions is to be found.

Where are those definitions for my success come from?

Are those the wishes of parents or other people?

If we attach our success only to material things, we can easily be frustrated and perhaps also fail. We can be dissatisfied, because always someone has a nicer car or a larger house. Because he is longer on vacation or always dressed perfectly. Even the suspicion that someone might have more often makes us uneasy when we focus only on material things.

But if we define success as a condition that occurs as soon as we have started something, we already have a success with the "start" shot. We can build on this "start-up success" and success.

Success can also mean for us that we have learned a lesson from something and do not make this avoidable error on the next attempt.

Success is also to rise once more often than we fall.

How often does a child fall before it can run properly? Do we then give him three more trials and then stamp it as a failure for the rest of his life? Hardly likely.

Success is also when we have embarked on a wrong path, which we recognize, rethink, turn around and try again.

The only way to fail is to give up (because the current obstacles seem too powerful), although the goals are really important to us. Even in this case, we can postpone the project to a later date and continue as the conditions improve. Even then it is again a success of the realization.

So, you see, it is not so easy to fail when we change our rating system, our benchmarks, and views. We can thereby feel successful in almost every situation and build further success on it. Write down your revised views into your "Book of Life" and write down a few successful actions of the last days. Always think about expanding your personal success database.

Personal success ritual

We have already discussed in the chapter "Your own focus" that our mood depends on our environment, among other things. However, we should pay attention to making our mood dependent on ourselves and thus to influence our environment positively. This in turn leads to a desired, positive feedback from the environment.

If we have experienced something wonderful, a success, then we are in a good mood. At this moment, it does not matter to us whether it rains, whether the children are arguing or whether some things do not work. At least for a certain time. The duration of this state of immunity is dependent on us, we establish this and can train this condition.

We must acquire certain patterns of behavior and see them as success if we adhere to them. The more frequently we follow these patterns, the better we manage to go through life, unaffected by external circumstances. But, like everything else, it has to be trained, otherwise it will not work.

A strange example: A trained behavior pattern is, for example, the stop before the red traffic light. If you do not do this and drive over the traffic light at red, there is a risk that you will be causing an accident and causing anger. In this case, you also know that you have behaved incorrectly. This annoys you even more because you can scold about the other as loud as you want.

However, if you stop at Red, and someone drives you from behind into the car, then you also have anger, but you know: They have behaved correctly. This makes things a bit less serious, because you have behaved correctly and that is a success in your eyes.

Despite unpleasant circumstances, you were successful in your cause. They stopped at red.

This is the part you can always contribute to the success of the cause. No matter what else happens, you have behaved as you think it is right and successful.

Let us transfer the extreme example of the traffic light to the daily life. It is only up to us whether we are friendly or not, whatever happens around us. We are always free to give a small, honest smile and to spread positive spirits, regardless of any external influences. It is a success for you if you can remain friendly in critical situations.

So, when we meet our personal success ritual, we are always successful in our eyes, and then we can't do much more. There are just a lot of situations that would have put us in a bad mood.

If you continually apply your personal success criterion, you will soon find that the people in your environment are responding. You do not give your opponent any reason to interfere with you through your own attitude. But more importantly, you can be absolutely certain of your cause. Even if attacks should come, you have done your utmost. Work every day to refine the ritual and apply it as often as possible.

What framework can we create for ourselves on a daily basis? Simply put, how does our daily ritual look like? In effect, there are measures to ensure compliance with a simple law:

Do not hurt anyone, not even yourself!

It comes from the Hunza, a tribe in Pakistan. Supposedly, it was originally their only law.

Think about it a few seconds. I have not found a situation so far that would not have helped. Of course, not all problems and conflicts are solved immediately, because the causes and the mutual injuries are already far in the past and can't be reversed. Nevertheless, everyone can try to define and train certain behaviours as of today, so that we can apply them a few times a day.

My success ritual includes the following points:

> Smile at my own mirror imagine each morning for one minute, make funny faces while stretching.

> Let peace take place every morning for a few minutes, thinking about all plans of the day.

> Ask myself the question: What can I do today to make myself feel successful?

> Check my energy level for friends, excitement and get my power started.

> Not letting myself get annoyed, not accepting the "gift"

> Always leave on good terms from my side.

> Strengthen my beliefs that there is enough for everyone.

> Leave the pleasure of "having found the solution on one's own" to the other person.

> Making everyone who meets me a little happy, at least giving them a smile.

> Treating myself and my family with love.

Make it a personal ritual and get yourself into the mood every day with which you are able to keep your part for a pleasant day. Remember the phrase "Do not hurt anyone, not even yourself." See the daily ritual as your success and build the day on this success.

Realizing success

Count your moments of happiness and see what you have. You are, for example, financially successful, have a great family and are completely healthy. It is time to be aware of this, to look forward to celebrating success and rewarding yourself. Buy something from your salary increase, go out to a nice place with your wife or give your employees a bonus.

To give a little happiness to oneself and others, not at some point in time, but in the moment of success, that is what matters. For one thing, you do not know what tomorrow is going to happen, maybe you are dead then. It does not make much sense to be the richest person in the cemetery. My father died at the age of 60 during a car accident. It can end faster than we think. I do not want to paint the devil on the wall, but what use is every effort and every success if they do not make our lives better.

If we are doing something good for ourselves at the moment of success, then we connect happiness moments with success. We want to have more and more moments of happiness, so our subconscious mind is looking for more success stories, because it knows: happiness moments are going to follow. This creates a solid emotional basis for further goals. Again, presented in another way: what are share profits good for if we do not use at least a part of it and do something good for us?

Money usually makes you happy only in two moments: when you get it and when you spend it for something beautiful again. In between, we often even worry. Worrying about losing it, worrying about having it not optimally designed, worrying about having to pay tax. All the worries cost us a lot of our valuable time again, which makes us even more worried. I know there are worse worries than having too much money, but a proverb says, "What you do not use, you will lose." This is also valid for money, time and success.

Document your life

What have we done in recent years? Time flies by so fast, the children grow bigger, we get older. Where does this time go?

Wherever it goes, I can't tell you, but I can tell you this. Write down the best experiences, actions, thoughts and successes daily or at least weekly. What did you do last weekend, for example? The fact that you have made a small mountain tour, you can even think of that after a little thought, but how great the joy of an e-mail of your best friend was, you have forgotten. Document your life. You invest so much time, energy, thoughts and money to master your life. You make so many experiences, good and bad, funny and sad. You always manage to get out of almost hopeless situations, and become ever stronger, wiser, even smarter. But all of this is no longer usable for anyone, we forget many experiences over time. No, we do not forget them, they are just no longer in our consciousness and hence also no longer available without the appropriate impulse. Let us create impulses in written form, to unfold our life in retrospect and to discover what actually happened.

While browsing through your diary, you will surely find many of the highlights of your life that you have not remembered for a long time. But you also read about low points and from the crisis. You collect your great moments in life, of which you can be proud. This collection will help you whenever you doubt yourself. You will be reminded of what you have achieved so far. Without knowing you, I know you have done a whole series of outstanding things. It can also be very small things, what is important is: you are or were proud of it. Collect these memories and write them into your "Book of Life". Mark the best experiences, wisdom, etc. every month, or summarize them briefly on one page. They will see what fun it is to fly over them again and again. Especially in times of self-doubt and crises, you can find strength, energy and surely also some hints that help you get out of the current situation quickly. Should you have children, it is additionally a very valuable gift to them. They can at any time read what challenges their mother or father had to face and how they did it. Perhaps it also says why they have done this and that. I would be glad to have such a book from my parents.

Spiral of success

Our potential, which is available to us as human beings, is gigantic. People are able to develop enormous power under certain conditions. Everyone has already heard of examples where someone was rescued by an extreme performance of another. I can confirm the tremendous powers of physical and mental nature released here when I remember the incredible power of my wife squeezing my hand at the birth of our first child. This happened at the birth of the child, when many hours of great exertion laid behind her.

In extreme situations, focus, emotion, thought and action are combined – and that means that at this moment we are literally able to move mountains. There is no room for distraction and doubt in these moments.

Unfortunately, we only use this potential to a very small extent in everyday life.

From this used part of our potential we take the energy for our actions. Depending on how much energy is available, the quality of our action is sometimes better and sometimes worse.

Simply put, you fill up just a small water bottle at the oasis and then go on expedition to the desert. Everyone is immediately aware that you will not get far. The success of the expedition will not be very great. You may be able to spend a day in the sun with it, but then you need much longer to recover from the trip. The result is not particularly satisfactory. You are frustrated and do not believe in success. If you do not believe in your success, then you will use even less of your potential on the next attempt, because it does not make sense in your eyes anyway.

Now the comparison with the water bottle is so simple that you will naturally immediately and legitimately think, then I take just more water with. This is absolutely true, we do not often do it, because we prefer to push the cause of our failure to the desert, the sun, the heat and the steep dunes.

However, if we admit that the reason for our failure was the low water supply, the solution becomes clear to us quickly. We take more water with us and we get much further. This means we are acting stronger, we are investing more strength in our project. However, we only invest more when we manage to see the small excursion with the small bottle of water as a test and thus also as a success.

Hurray, we have a success story, and that now we know what we have to look out for.

This makes us even more inclined to our goal of reaching the next oasis, and therefore encourages us to draw more from our potential.

Even though it may still not be possible in the second run with more water, we have gone a long way further than in the first attempt. This strengthens our faith in being able to do it. Furthermore, we have realized that we can no longer carry water on our shoulders, since otherwise we would not be able to make the route for conditional reasons.

We see this realization as a success again and think further. We change the system and take camels as bearers. Again, we are investing on the basis of small successes.

Behold, we are suddenly in a position where we have to go through whole deserts. We are very enthusiastic, and we are conscious of the fact that we are able to do everything in the future. We believe in our success and that is why we can use even more of our skills and act more and more for new adventures. At some point, we come across the sea and find that camels can't swim well. We are developing ships and crossing the seas ... (so we would have explained a part of human history at the same time).

An ascending success story has developed which leads you from success to success. This happens preferably when you set your definition for success so that even a supposed failure is a success and you learn something from the matter to make it better on the next run. If the causes of failure are not properly analyzed and viewed neutrally, there is a great danger of failing again next time. Who can help you?

KEY 21

COACHING

Do you have a golfing or a tennis coach? Do yoga or Zumba under expert guidance? Do your children have a piano teacher, flute lessons, riding lessons or anything else?

Do you have a coach for your life, for the challenges that are waiting for you every day? Somebody who gives you feedback and corrects your technique? Anyone who correctly analyzes the causes of your failure?

Why not? Where do you take the time to find your way, often using the "trial and error" method? How do you know that you are not "operating blind"?

This sounds a bit arrogant, of course, and I know from my own experience that in the vortex of life, you often just try to keep your head above water.

Our life does not consist of a discipline but is very complex. We do not need a coach but several. We need them in different areas, at different doses, at different times and in varying intensity.

THE all inclusive success coach, we will not find

In this book, I have presented many areas that are fundamental to a holistic and sustainable success. All these points can be improved on your own and you will be much more successful than before. The interaction, the synergy of the individual themes, is decisive. This can be done much more easily by adding external help in the form of a coach.

We know what it takes to live our own visions and build a solid foundation of abilities and contacts. We can achieve a lot with this and above all we can better recognize and describe our deficits. Shortcomings in the current moment and uncertainties in the direction we have taken.

A different perspective on our challenges now allows a third person to recognize the things that hinder us from happening, often much more quickly than we do. A suitable coach gives the decisive stimulus or adds the final puzzle pieces.

Thus, we save time and gain confidence that we are on the right way.

Frequently, a friend is a useful coach, if he is honest with us. Better, however, is someone who is an expert in his field, which we respect and from which we also accept suggestions. It is important that we determine ourselves in which areas we are

Trainers take. Because a trainer is an expert in a field and not a flat-rate life counseling.

We have to decide which topics we want to edit and then we should choose the best coach for this. If we describe him or her as closely as possible to our challenges and our goals, this results in goal-oriented, effective coaching, which in turn results in countable results.

Good results mean success. Success is "profit" in the form of more money, more time, greater health and more joy. Whatever your "profit", you gain new perspectives through the coaching and thus the possibilities to improve certain fields.

The investment for the right coach pays off very quickly. Often, they are supposed to be small things that let the stone start rolling. Be it through a new idea or a better name for your new product.

I've had about 15 different business cards and slogans made over the years, until I finally found the wording, with a coach, that is authentic to me and believes in what I really stand for. I notice clearly that the wording finally fits, because I like to tell everyone about it.

It was a lengthy process of finding where I initially did everything myself and knew everything better – with unsatisfactory results. In the second step, I have everything

"Experts", but without precise specifications, because I wanted to rely on their expertise and creativity. Accordingly, these results were also unsatisfactory. Ultimately, I turned to a first-class coach and a 20-minute conversation with him led to the appropriate name and slogan. Since then, synergies and successes have emerged where I would never have expected them. It just gets better.

I am not only referring to coaching, but to the entire process that I describe in this book. It is important to first gain an overview, to set priorities, and to make improvements on a selective and continuous basis. It was only this initial situation that enabled me to pinpoint my intentions and to describe how a twenty-minute coaching session could bring about a breakthrough.

An external coach or consultant will take you back on track at the right time or give you momentum and confidence when you have stalled. It will give you impulses that you will not be able to come to for a long time, and you will win money and time. In addition to the specialist area, your coach can help you to put the positive things in a bright light and achieve the successes so far.

Decide who can be of use to you NOW and determine what you want to improve first. The best coaches get the best athletes to get even better. But they are very different, if you need support in the area of strength, endurance, nutrition or the mental area.

Look for someone who will allow you to praise, but who also corrects you. Someone you pay for his performance and who appreciates and improves your performance. In addition, you should constantly continue the process of analysis, as the next challenge may be solved better with another coach.

Problem solving

Another challenge is often the issue of "problem solving." When it comes to problems, most people waste most of their energy and time on describing the problem, complaining about it, and especially thinking about it. They focus on the problem by all means rather than on the solution. Do you remember the stone on the ski slope in the "Focus" section? As if by magic, I have hit it with the new ski.

Changing this focus is anything but easy. Therefore, a coach is also recommended to help us take a different angle of view. First, however, it is important to develop self-willingness to solve the "problem".

Watch your next problem and pay attention to the questions that hover around in your head. Are they solution-oriented or problem-oriented? How much time do you spend thinking about the problem, describing it to others in all its colors and with all its consequences, in order to get even more angry about it? How much energy do you use for the actual solution?

Let the word "problem" consciously affect you for a moment. How does that feel? Normally, we are so conditioned that the word is negatively associated. Even this subconscious negative occupancy builds up a resistance in us. No one wants problems. Just replace the word against "challenge". For many, this word is rather positive. Speak of challenges when it comes to problems. Because we accept challenges, we can be challenged and can show our strength.

Then you begin to spend your time with the challenge, using the power of the question again. First, define the topic that is going to challenge you, and find the true core, the cause.

The following questions serve a solution-oriented approach. The combination of the question I have seen for the first time with Tony Robbins Personal Power, tried, slightly modified and felt as very useful. Under the questions I have written again a few own answers as an example.

What is not optimal now?

The formulation assumes that you know a state that is better. Otherwise you would not know that something is not optimal. Imagine the desired final state and describe it.

> I earn too little money and have too little time, which frustrates me. If I made more money, I could pay better teachers for my children and I would be much more relaxed, would be a better father and spend more time with my family ...

What is good about this situation?

If there is really nothing good, then ask what could be the good thing when I look 10 years into the future? You know the sentence: "Somehow we look back and then everything seems to have been funny". Try it right away, put 10 years into the future and then look back from this perspective, back to the present day, to the current situation. Do you think you can still remember this situation in ten years? –I have forcibly revised my old-age provision, structured it better, and greatly reduced my running costs.

What do I need to do so that I will not be confronted with such challenges in the future?

Do I need more skills, should I organize myself better? Is it time to treat my environment differently?

> ❯ Regularly check the measures for success. Measure whether I get closer to the goal or remove myself from it. From this, develop and carry out the necessary course corrections.

What will I stop doing now, so that I will not be faced with such challenges in the future?

What kind of behavior do I have in such situations? What or who should I keep?

> ❯ Unclear objectives; Too many distractions by trying to find confirmation in others; To doubt me and my abilities.

How can I now find an efficient and successful resolution for the upcoming challenge and enjoy the solution process?

To do this, imagine the desired final state and write down the ideas that come to your mind. Begin immediately with the implementation, at least with a small thing, so that things get moving.

> ❯ How can I make more money in less time? How do I do this with my existing skills and resources. Create a product, write a book, and

share your knowledge and experience so that it will benefit many people. Money is a measure of the value one gives to the other. Do this at beautiful places and enjoy writing. Sell it - and the income flows independently of your time.

From the answers to these questions, you develop your solution strategy. Depending on how big the challenge is, you go through the individual steps, as described in the book. If you do not feel like this, check your current power level from zero to ten. In the meantime, you know some ways to overcome your inner pig dog and put yourself in the necessary mood so that you can successfully counter any challenge.

Make sure you spend 90% of your time finding and implementing solutions. Only about 10% you should use on self-compassion, thought-proving games and the search for confirmation of the "wrong". You will see how unspectacular many challenges can be solved and how much time you will gain for other things and new goals.

Significantly, many people do not want to, because they suddenly have too much time they don't know anything to do with. Besides, it seems as if they have no problems. What should they talk about with the others, in the many hours when their own problems and those of the others were discussed in endless loops. In addition, they feel they are no longer important when they do not have any problems. This mountain, made visible to all, gives many people a right to exist and the possibility to be stressed. Remember, in our society, it is important to know who is stressful and important, and we are all very important. In our conditioned concept, this means that we also have many important things to do. When we do important things, we hope for recognition, praise and gratitude. Who would not do that? If we also play the joy of the commendation to the outside, we feel it clearly in ourselves. This joy is the little flame, the inner child, which wants to radiate properly again. Re-discover your feelings, literally "take the blanket away", and rejoice that the inner strength will help you to use the time you have chosen to achieve YOUR goals. You don't want to outsource your problems and be more successful in solving your challenges. This makes a lot more impression, especially on yourself. You will find that your friends, colleagues and new acquaintances will soon be conducting quite different conversations with you, which will lead you back in your development. There will surely be some conversation partners, because there will be no "problems" more to discuss any longer, which again leads to more time. Stand to yourself and decide what is important in your life. If you would like to go back to the chapter "Important is relative", please take a coach who can accompany you on your way.

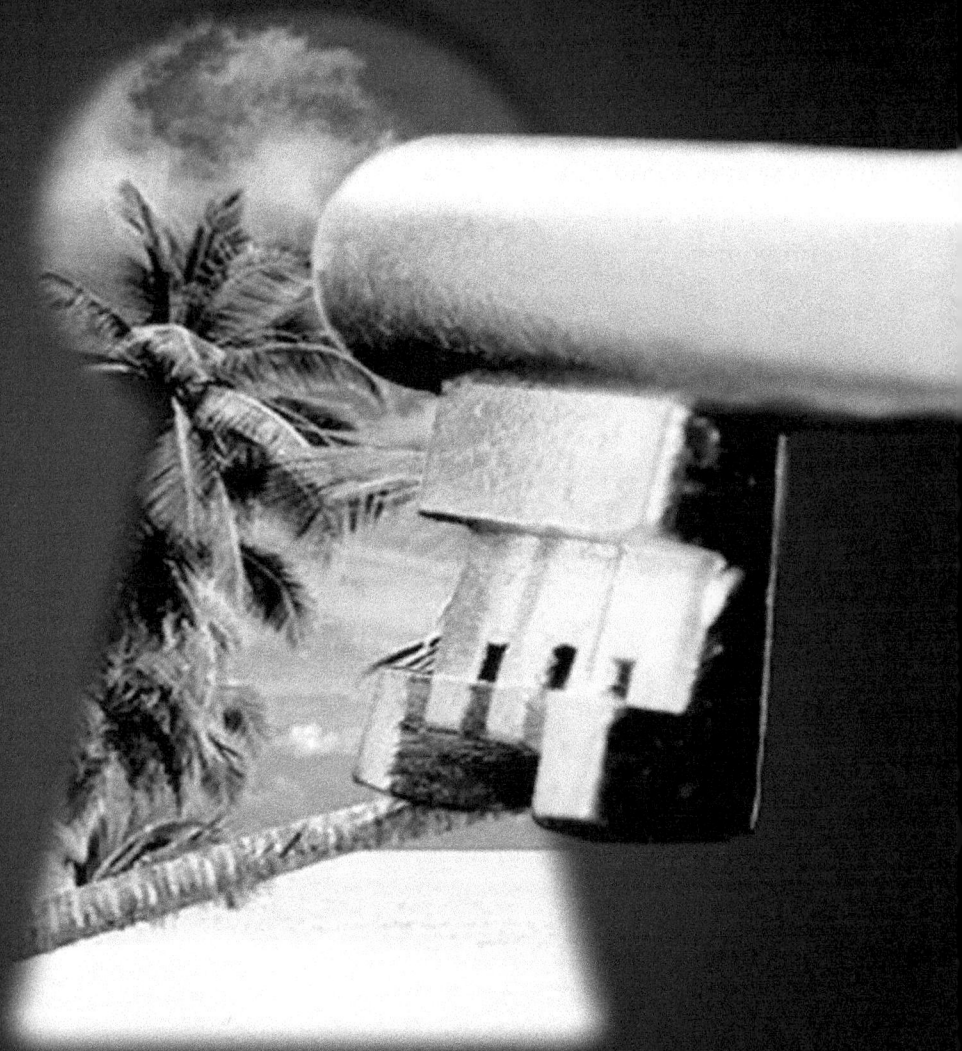

IN THE END – PEACE AND CONFIDENCE

If self-doubt, anxiety, frustration, and excessive demands were your companions for a long time, they now more and more deviate from the deep inner peace. The moment I knew and also felt exactly what I wanted, what my passion was, the rest came automatically. Suddenly, all previous efforts and deeds intertwine. Nothing seems to have been in vain. Perhaps similar to the sailors of past centuries, who suddenly felt unconsciously in the open sea after weeks, but maintained the direction and were heading for it. Slowly, the signs of the near land were growing. Birds emerged, flotsam was sighted more frequently, the waves changed until finally, on the horizon, land was in sight, which they soon reached.

Far before, however, after many exertions, hardships and difficulties, everything is quiet, there is no longer any pressure. Everything seems to run automatically. I am living the game as a spectator, who is relaxed and full of joy doing his tasks. The visions become tangible, more and more often I am dreaming of a wonderful present and future in daydreams. There is no longer any doubt, only the joy and enthusiasm with which the tasks are done. Each action leads to a further expansion of visions, and reality is coming more and more closer to my goals of the original version by reaching my goals. I feel very good about it,

I am happy to be able to help others with my knowledge, and therefore I can also wonder the rewards of life for this. At the same time, rest returns and all pressure seems to fall off, even though I am in the middle of the process.

What has to be done now? For me, only left to say is: "Slowly ahead!". The sails are set, the target is clear, check the course. Take care of your guests and give them an outstanding "journey", an outstanding lecture, a sustainable seminar or a groundbreaking coaching.

Thank you

Finally, I would like to thank you and congratulate you. You are among the few people who not only think about changes, but also begin to act. I wish you all the best on your way to your outstanding life, much joy and many successes. Remember to do your best, also in bad times, even if it may be anything but easy. Browse through this book again and again, perhaps you'll see things from a different angle, or discover new ways to reach your goals even better. But above all: celebrate and document your successes, as well as reading this book.

www.ingramcontent.com/pod-product-compliance
Lightning Source LLC
Chambersburg PA
CBHW030314220326
41519CB00068B/3042